LIBRARY
NSCC, WATERFR
80 MAWIO'MI PLAC
DARTMOUTH, NS

U J Г
C6 101
K53
2004

Me to We

TURNING SELF-HELP
ON ITS HEAD

Please return to:
Organizational Learning
Nova Scotia Community College
5685 Leeds Street, PO Box 1153
Halifax NS B3J 2X1

Me to We

TURNING SELF-HELP
ON ITS HEAD

CRAIG KIELBURGER & MARC KIELBURGER

John Wiley & Sons Canada Ltd.

Copyright © 2004 by Craig Kielburger and Marc Kielburger

All rights reserved. No part of this work covered by the copyright
herein may be reproduced or used in any form or by any
means—graphic, electronic, or mechanical without the prior
written permission of the publisher. Any request for photocopying,
recording, taping, or information storage and retrieval systems of
any part of this book shall be directed in writing to The Canadian
Copyright Licensing Agency (Access Copyright). For an Access
Copyright license, visit www.accesscopyright.ca or call toll free
1-800-893-5777.

Care has been taken to trace ownership of copyright material
contained in this book. The publisher will gladly receive any
information that will enable them to rectify any reference or
credit line in subsequent editions.

Library and Archives of Canada Cataloguing in Publication
Kielburger, Craig, 1982-
    Me to we : turning self-help on it's head / Craig Kielburger,
    Marc Kielburger.

Includes index.
ISBN 0-470-83510-9

1. Altruism.   2. Helping behavior.   3. Community development.
4. Self-actualization (Psychology)   I. Kielburger, Marc II. Title.
BF637.H4K53 2004   177'.7   C2004-902930-4

Production Credits:
Cover design: Ian Koo
Interior text design: Ian Koo, Adrian So R.G.D.
Front cover and author photograph: Pi Media Partners
Printer: Transcontinental Printing Inc.

Printed in Canada
10 9 8 7 6 5 4 3

To our parents
for their love and support.

Contents

Preface ix

Chapter 1: Two Worlds 1

My Story: Kim Phuc 11

Chapter 2: Our Self-Help Culture: Fool's Gold 15

My Story: Keith Taylor 25

Chapter 3: Our Self-Help Culture:
  Happiness in a Bubble 31

My Story: Tim Lefens 43

Chapter 4: Me to We (from Us) 47

My Story: Archbishop Desmond Tutu
  and Jonathan White 61

Chapter 5: The Roots of Self-Help 65

My Story: Richard Gere 77

Chapter 6: The *Minga* and Community 81

My Story: Dr. Jane Goodall 97

Chapter 7: Searching for Meaning, Happiness,
  and Success 99

My Story: Oprah Winfrey 113

Chapter 8: Within "We" Is "Me"   117

My Story: Kathy Buckley   127

Chapter 9: Helping Others Is Good for You   133

My Story: John Gaither and Jordana Weiss   147

Chapter 10: Help Yourself to a Better
World: Join the Movement   155

My Story: Lindsay Avner   165

Chapter 11: Be the Change You Want to See   169

My Story: Joe Opatowski   187

Chapter 12: Writing Your Own Story   191

My Story: Anonymous   201

Stories, Facts, and Actions   203

About the Contributors   213

About the Authors   218

Free the Children   219

Leaders Today   220

Acknowledgments   221

Endnotes   223

Index   237

Still Want to Learn More?   244

Preface

Dear Reader,

The Amazon.com website lists 51,603 books under the keyword search for "The Secret of Happiness." Apparently, it's no longer a secret. Many of these books feature programs with four, five, eight steps, ten potent questions, and 72-hour guaranteed results. We, on the other hand, offer you one solution—one habit to being *happy*. If you think there should be more steps in a book this size, don't worry; it's a *really* good step. We're going to turn self-help on its head!

You may be thinking that we are rather young to be writing a book like this. That may be, but being young sometimes means that you come up with new ways of looking at things. At an early age, we discovered a simple truth that changed our lives, and we wanted to share it with you.

So, who are we? We are two brothers from a middle-class suburban neighborhood who grew up with a love for volunteering and being socially involved. In 1995, we founded *Free the Children*, an organization committed to bringing education to children overseas, and through this work we have been blessed with some extraordinary life experiences. We have had the opportunity to travel the world, visiting more than 40 countries. Along the way, we have shared simple meals of rice and roti with people struggling in the slums of Calcutta, and have also attended opulent banquets with some of the world's most powerful business moguls at the World Economic Forum, in Davos, Switzerland. In the war-torn villages of Sierra Leone, we've had discussions with people whose limbs were savagely amputated by armed militias, and at major United Nations conferences, we've sat on panels with heads of state and royalty. We've spent hours playing and talking with hundreds of street children from Brazil to Thailand who have no guardians in their lives, as well as meeting with tens of thousands of students, parents, and educators in schools around the world.

And in the process we found the most surprising thing; the people we least expected to be happy were some of the happiest.

We made another surprising discovery. Our lives changed as we set out to learn more about other cultures and people we encountered. Upon returning to North America, we were frequently invited to speak at motivational seminars and conferences, where people gathered to discuss different paths to happiness and peace. We found ourselves sitting on panels with people selling quick and easy solutions to life's struggles. The more we listened to them celebrate power and money, however, the more we began to see that their solutions conflicted with what we had witnessed in our service work, both at home and overseas.

Since its inception, Free the Children has grown into an international movement of children helping children that has improved the lives of over a million children in more than 35 countries. The organization has built over 400 schools to date and provides clean water and medical supplies, and establishes women's cooperatives. In 1998, we started Leaders Today, a leadership institute that empowers and inspires over 250,000 youth every year in North America and around the world to become actively involved in volunteerism, service to others, and bettering the world. We have seen the impact of these efforts in the communities where we have worked, in the young people and adults who have been transformed by helping others, and also in our own lives.

Being involved in this work has made us happier than we'd ever imagined, happier than two guys possibly have the right to be. And those around us, friends, family, and colleagues who have stepped outside of themselves, and changed their lives tell us that they are happy, too.

Could it be we have found the secret to happiness? We think we have.

We drew the inspiration to write this book from our volunteer work and travels. The road that we have traveled and the people we have met have led us to one shockingly simple conclusion: being thinner, smarter, richer, faster, or having better abs, will not make you happy, despite claims to the contrary. In fact, this book challenges the notion that self-help—worrying and fretting about yourself all the time, focusing solely on yourself, is the best way to improve your life. It invites you to find happiness and purpose by reaching out to others.

This reverse path led to a book that is a fundamental departure from most books in the modern self-help industry. It represents a complete shift in approach—in its purpose, its structure, and its message. We published it straight to soft cover for a reason: we wanted to make it as financially accessible as possible.

Friends contributed their own stories that are included between chapters as examples of personal and social change they experienced in their own lives. Their stories are not to be taken merely as bedtime heart warmers. Statistics and actions about the social issues discussed in the stories are available in the appendix for you to use as your springboard to a better life, and a better world.

A different type of map leads you along a path less traveled. After you've discovered and absorbed the ideas presented in this book, your life may not end up as you had envisioned. You may not acquire a house on a beach in the Caymans, but you may often find your toes grounded in the sand. You may not see an enormous change in your social life, but in your life you may very well see enormous social change. You may not find the person of your dreams, but you will help young people go beyond theirs. You may not retire with a gold watch, but you will think of this time of your life as golden years.

This book is designed to start a movement, to bring about a *revolution* in giving and community building. We will not measure the impact of this book in sales, but in the number of people motivated to reach out to others, because we will have succeeded not when you buy this book, but when you *use it and pass it on to someone else.* We promise above all that it will open your eyes and challenge the way you look at life. And it *will* change your life and the lives of everyone you meet. We wrote this book because we believe in its message: one small step for kindness, one large step for humankind.

Let us begin.
Craig and Marc

Chapter 1:

TWO WORLDS

"Not until we are lost do we begin to understand ourselves."
– Henry David Thoreau –
(1817–1862)
Philosopher

It was like visiting the home of a friend. We knocked on the door and were immediately invited in. We were expecting a guard out front or a large sign, but neither was present. Dozens of people dressed in white were moving about their daily tasks; the floor had been worn smooth by the footsteps of visitors. A ceiling fan was not sufficient to ward off the intense heat. We had heard so much about this place and the woman who had started it all. We were initially told she was not accepting visitors and we should come back tomorrow. Disappointed, we prepared to leave. However, at that moment, she entered the room.

She was much smaller in stature than we had expected. As she came our way, we saw that her features were plain, old, and wrinkled, but her face glowed. Her calloused fingers immediately reached out to us and we were surprised to feel their warmth and strength as she took our hands into hers. She smiled and looked into our eyes as if she were searching for our souls. In spite of her many responsibilities and busy schedule, she was in no hurry to leave; she took the time to meet with us–to be present.

Our meeting with this remarkable woman, named Agnes, taught us important lessons that were destined to help shape our lives. She was born in Skopje, Yugoslavia, now Macedonia, in Eastern Europe. At the age of 12, she decided to devote her life to her religious beliefs. Six years later, she was stationed to teach at a private school in one of the poorest cities in South Asia, where she would work for nearly two decades. Over the years, she often heard the desperate cries of hungry and sick people coming from the alleyways near the school. She could not help because she was ordered not to leave the compound where she taught.

One day, however, Agnes became seriously ill with tuberculosis. Like many people who are faced with illness and possible death, she began to reflect more deeply on the meaning of her life. On a fateful train ride to Darjeeling, where she was sent for rest and recuperation, she began to ask herself some questions. Who was she meant to be? What was her purpose? How did she want to live the rest of her life? She made life-changing decisions that day. She had reached a turning point, something that jolted her out of her reality and revealed a more meaningful path.

It wasn't long after returning home that Agnes was forced to put her resolution into action. She came across an elderly woman who was abandoned and dying on the street. Agnes picked the woman up and took her to the closest hospital for medical attention, but the facility refused to treat the dying woman because she had no money. Agnes took her to the next hospital, and the next, with no success in finding someone to help. So Agnes brought the woman back to her own home, laid her down in a warm bed, and stayed by her side, reassuring her and caring for her until, soon, afterwards, the woman passed away. At that point, Agnes made a conscious choice to dedicate her life to helping the poorest of the poor to live and die with dignity, respect, and love. She founded the Missionaries of Charity in Calcutta, a new order of nuns whose purpose was to care for those who had no one to care for them—the dying, the disabled, the destitute, and the orphaned. She became known around the world as Mother Teresa, the name she chose when she took her vows as a nun.

In 1969, a documentary focused the eyes of the world on her saintly work but she did not let the attention she received go to her head. She tore out the plush carpet donated for one of the homes of her sisters and gave it to the poor. She rejected the traditional elaborate banquet when she won the Nobel Peace Prize in 1979, and insisted that the money be used to feed the homeless. Her convent was a simple dwelling with only the barest of necessities, tucked away on an unassuming side street in Calcutta.

We spent precious moments with Mother Teresa that day. When we asked her how she maintained her hope surrounded by an overwhelming number of sick and dying people, she humbly responded: "They die one at a time, and so I save them one at a time." She gently touched us on the shoulder and urged us never to lose hope. She told us that every day each one of us receives a calling to reach out and help others, and that we have a choice to help or not to help. "In our lives, we can do no great things," she said, "only small things with great love."

As we left the convent, the dismal streets took on a different, almost hopeful light. Mother Teresa's message of steady and unyielding compassion seemed to open up a path through the poverty and sickness that characterized so much of the city. Her vision was compelling not only because of what she had accomplished for others, but also because of who she was as a person. She was proof that through small meaningful actions, one after another, people *can* change the world. It was a powerful lesson that would immensely affect our lives as we continued to move forward in our own work.

People sometimes question the idea of looking to Mother Teresa as a role model. "Our lives are different," people often say. "We have other responsibilities." We live in a different reality. Some even speak of being paralyzed by a "Mother Teresa syndrome," a feeling that few could ever reach this level of service and goodness.

However, Mother Teresa was not simply a kind little old nun living in the slums of Calcutta. She was also a quintessential entrepreneur and leader who saw something wrong in her surroundings and took action to change the situation one step at a time. She built a huge organization in the most challenging of circumstances, formulated its constitution, and established more than 500 centers in 120 countries, including one of the first hospices for AIDS victims in New York City and others in Atlanta and San Francisco. The purpose of her organization was to care for those forgotten by society, and her message of simple service, small actions, and deep love resonated around the world.

After meeting Mother Teresa and other great leaders and social justice heroes over the past decade, we've realized that while they are extraordinary individuals, what matters more is that they are all human. They are flesh and blood, made of the same substance as all of us. Mother Teresa's journals reveal that even she went through periods of self-doubt and criticism. What set this woman apart was the way in which she sought to overcome her insecurities and improve her life, not by closing herself off from others, but by opening herself to them.

Coming home from the Calcutta slums, we wondered how Mother Teresa's life would be judged by the standards of our North American society. The values that guided her seem to stand in stark contrast to the goals set by much of today's Western culture, which focus on "getting ahead," "looking out for number one," and "helping yourself." Her life would fall short of the brand of "success" and "happiness" that is defined by these goals: she did not own many possessions; she was not wealthy and did not have a lot of political clout; she was not "beautiful" in the way that beauty is depicted on the covers of fashion magazines. To many of us, Mother Teresa's selflessness seemed to strip her life of all of its pleasures and comforts. We wonder how she could possibly have been happy.

It all depends, of course, on how we define happiness. Today, North America is at its wealthiest point in history. According to the goals set by previous generations, millions of us have it made—with a car in (almost) every driveway, a chicken in (almost) every pot—most of us should now not only be happy, we should be downright ecstatic and dancing in the streets. But many of us are not putting on those dancing shoes quite yet. For great numbers of people, the quest for happiness and fulfillment often gets lost in the rush and daily details of our complex lives. We lose sight of our purpose and direction under the weight of in-boxes, bills, and day-planners. Sometimes, we prefer to leave the search for the meaning of life to philosophers or religious leaders. Focused on keeping our eyes on "the road," "the ball," or "the prize"—we forget to pause and ask ourselves what exactly we are chasing after. After a visit to North America, Mother Teresa once observed that she had never seen such an abundance of material things. But she had also never seen "such a poverty of the spirit, of loneliness, and of being unwanted." In her eyes, this spiritual poverty was worse than the physical poverty of people in the Calcutta slums.

Like Mother Teresa, many of us find periods in our own lives when we question our existence and purpose. Who am I? Who do I want to become? What do I want to do with my life? Often we feel lost, uncertain, or stressed by the speed of life. The guidelines by which previous generations lived do not always match our current situation, and the social problems of our time have added to the breakdown of family and community support, leaving millions of us searching for greater meaning.

I LOST MYSELF ON THE SHELF

"We excel at making a living but often fail at making a life.
We celebrate our prosperity but yearn for purpose.
We cherish our freedoms but long for connection.
In an age of plenty, we feel spiritual hunger."[1]
— David G. Myers —
(b. 1942)
Professor of Psychology

In their search for happiness, millions of people are turning to the self-help industry for guidance. Some believe that they will be happy if they have more—more money, more beauty, more popularity. Others search for more insight and inspiration. A never-ending quest for self-fulfillment has North Americans reaching for their credit cards. And there are legions of people offering to help them solve every conceivable problem in life. The Amazon.com website turns up 162,179 titles under the heading "Self-Help," offering advice on everything from weight-loss to financial mastery, time management, memory improvement, self-hypnosis, personal transformation, finding your inner child, reviving your spirituality, and boosting your creativity and self-esteem. Motivational books, CDs, and self-growth seminars are an annual $5.7 billion US business, with percentage growth in the double digits.[2]

In the industry's greatest coup, the venerable *New York Times* added a new category to its best-seller list, "Advice." The move was precipitated by the sheer numbers of new guides to fulfillment, happiness, and "The New You" muscling out the shelf space of traditional non-fiction books such as biographies, memoirs, and political commentaries.

In 1999, $588 million worth of these books was sold in the United States, and more and more publishers are recognizing the lucrative potential of the self-help market. A recent article in *The Economist* reported the launch of a new line of personal development books by a well-known international publishing house. Called "Momentum," the series is being promoted as a "completely new publishing philosophy that revolves around one thing: you."[3] The article suggests that even though a successful self-help industry should logically put itself out of business, based on the soaring popularity of these books, this is not likely to happen.

What is driving the demand for self-help literature? We believe that the breakdown of support systems we once had in our families and communities, along with the rise of our consumer-driven society, have left millions of us searching for meaning in our lives. The interest in self-help underlines the questions nagging at our souls, the issues deep in our hearts that we hide even from our friends, and the goals that we set for our society and ourselves. "Self-help books are fantastically important," notes Peter York, social observer and author, "because they tell you what America or Britain is worrying about."[4] It is often said that in order to understand an era, you must examine the literature of its time. Based on book sales, it is arguable that self-help has become the literature of our time. It represents the values and the concerns that occupy our minds.

No matter the type of self-help—whether it pertains to business, relationships, or physical well-being—we follow these programs because we seek happiness through an improved life. More than simply mirroring our priorities, self-help books serve as the maps and compasses that guide us toward success, happiness, and personal fulfillment. As such, they redefine how we understand these terms.

The problem is that many self-help books promote extrinsic goals such as money, power, and physical attractiveness as the keys to happiness, despite extensive psychological evidence that real happiness lies in establishing close relationships, community-building, and the contribution one makes to society.[5] By promoting individualism and linking happiness and success to material possessions, much of the self-help industry only exacerbates the problems that lead people to look for help in the first place.

Many of the quick-fix schemes, plans, and parables for sale have one thing in common: what's good for "me"—and in most cases, only "me." This is the legacy of the "Me Generation" inspired by psychoanalyst Fritz Perls' doctrine of "I do my thing and you do yours."[6] The values of this era endure today, characterized by a desire to help only the self through an unbridled pursuit of wealth and a win-at-all-costs mentality. In today's world, many self-help manuals combine the components of "self" and "help," but ignore the other crucial element, namely, that the word "help" was once used primarily in relation to "others," and not solely for the self.

This is not to say that every self-help book on the market is unhelpful. There are some outstanding titles filled with seeds of truth, practical advice, and sound psychological insight on subjects such as healthy living, emotional health and maturity, parenting, or moral and spiritual renewal. However, more and more, it's becoming easier to distinguish between those books that are out to *help* and those that are out to *sell*.[7] Today, books featuring diet-fads, tips on how to snag a mate, and get-rich-quick schemes have come to dominate the self-help market. Amazon.com lists over 54,000 self-help diet books, 67,000 marriage advice books, and more than 90,000 money advice books. But when an estimated 65 percent of American adults are overweight or obese,[8] when the divorce rate has doubled since the 1960s,[9] and when the percentage of Americans living in poverty jumped from 11.7 percent in 2001 to 12.1 percent in 2002—representing nearly 34.6 million people, it seems that the advice may not be working.[10]

It's not simply that many self-help products do not deliver on their promises, but that they can be harmful to individuals and to society as a whole. The more we are encouraged to turn away from others in seeking our own path, the more isolated we become. In isolation, many of us choose products over people to help feel better about our lives but soon find ourselves searching for more. For a few individuals this might not seem to matter, but when people move this way en masse, it eats at the very soul of our society.

We believe that the self-help industry is contributing to the breeding of a self-help culture, in which the self is the only thing in focus, and individualism and material possessions are what millions have come to value above all else. We use the term "self-help culture" to describe these social trends for two reasons; firstly, because fundamental changes in family, community, and religious affiliations have pushed our society to become more self-focused and self-involved, and millions are now looking to help themselves, often at the expense of helping others; and secondly, because much of the self-help industry is the clearest manifestation of this phenomenon. This book uses the discussion of the self-help industry simply as a springboard to the broader argument of the failure of the modern western world's me-centered path to happiness. We will attempt not only to turn self-help on its head but also to question what makes us happy and what is best for society.

In order to achieve a true and lasting sense of success and happiness, it is necessary to deconstruct the many elements that have come to define our self-help culture and create a fundamental shift in our thinking. This may sound like a challenge, but it is one that will make us stronger. When we have the courage to question and move beyond what we know, we open ourselves up to new and more meaningful possibilities. For individuals and whole societies, this has always been the way of real progress and change.

We began this chapter by reflecting on our meeting with Mother Teresa who, according to the norms of our self-help culture, could never have lived a fulfilled and happy life. In our travels to the developing world we discovered that people of many other cultures, despite their lack of material wealth, are also very happy. We were very grateful for what they taught us, and our work over the past decade is a tribute to their courage and wisdom.

With this book, we wish to put forth an alternative path that we believe will transform your life. In the process, we will introduce you to a number of people who have already made this journey and who want to share their stories with you. You will find one of their reflections at the end of each chapter, starting with our friend, Kim.

My Story

KIM PHUC

I still can't look at the picture, not even today. It hurts too much.

That image of myself as a little girl in Vietnam, running with my arms hanging wide, naked, my skin on fire, my mouth open in terror and crying for help, the smoke all around me—it still is too powerful. I feel so *horrible* inside, like it's happening all over again. I can smell the burning, I can feel the heat, and deep it my soul, it hurts!

So I don't look. I keep the picture filed away, hidden from view.

But I don't feel hatred for that picture anymore. Instead, I feel grateful. To me, that picture is a gift.

It took a very, very long time for me to feel that way.

For many years, I was just The Girl in the Picture—and I hated it.

I had been photographed when I was nine years old and my village was hit by napalm. We were running on the highway, away from the explosions. The sky was red, as if heaven were on fire. I could not keep up with my brothers; they ran too fast. As I ran I turned to see an airplane flying low to the ground. I had never seen one so close before. I watched it drop four bombs into the swirling smoke. I kept running.

Suddenly, a force struck me from behind. I fell forward onto the ground. I did not know what I was doing when I pulled at the neck of my shirt. I just felt so hot. My burning clothes fell away from me. I looked at my left arm. It was covered with flames and brownish-black goo. I tried to wipe it off and yelled in pain as my hand began to burn too.

I knew I should catch up with my brothers but I felt so tired and so thirsty, like I was burning from the inside. "Oh Ma," I kept crying. "*Nong qua! Nong qua!*" Too hot! Too hot!

That's when the journalist took my picture.

I hardly remember what happened next. The journalists poured their canteens of water over my skin; it was falling off in pink and black chunks. The photographer got a poncho to cover me, then helped me into a van and drove me to the hospital in Saigon. The van swerved around refugees and with every bump I screamed in agony. The napalm had incinerated my ponytail and left my neck, my back, and my left arm a raw, mushy, oozing mess. It had killed my two cousins. I wished it had killed me too.

It wasn't until much later that I learned that the picture, taken by AP photographer Nick Ut, had been printed on the front pages of newspapers around the world and won him the Pulitzer Prize. It made Nick famous. It made me famous too, though I wished with all my heart it had not.

For the next 14 months I remained in an American hospital in Saigon, enduring many surgeries and painful procedures paid for by a private foundation. I had to relearn how to stand, walk, and feed and dress myself. Finally, recovered, I was sent back to my village to try to rebuild my life.

But my life would never be the same.

I could not take the hot sun on my unstable new skin nor the blowing dust in my damaged lungs. I suffered bad headaches and sudden, intense pain. My family was forced to live in a hot, airless house in the city as war raged around us. We had little money, not even for the ice I depended on for pain relief.

As the years went by, I remember as a teenager feeling so very ugly! I would look in the mirror at the scars that covered my body and ask "Why me?" I was able to hide my disfigurement by growing my hair long, wearing long sleeves, and resting my left arm on my hip so you couldn't tell it was shorter.

It was my shameful secret. Once, when I was 17, sitting at my desk waiting for the teacher to arrive, I heard some girls talking about a boy who had scars on his hands. "He is so handsome," one girl said. "Ooooh! Yuck!" the others chimed in. "Have you seen his scars? So ugly!"

The only thing that kept me going was my dream of becoming a doctor. I'd been so impressed with how the doctors had helped me; I wanted to help people too. I studied hard and was accepted into medical school. I was thrilled—but it was short-lived. A few months later, foreign journalists found me. They wanted to interview me 10 years after the war.

At first, I was flattered—me? Famous? But then the Vietnamese communist government took over, demanding that I act as their anti-capitalist poster girl, their symbol of the war. They told me what to say and do, watching my every move. They made me abandon medical school and be available to pose for the cameras. Outside, I was smiling; inside, I felt so sad, like I was a victim all over again. I could have no friends; it was too dangerous. They warned my parents that if something happened to me, they would go to prison.

In between media interviews, I went to the library, reading every book I could find on religion. I'd hoped that within those pages I would find some answers, some meaning for my life. There, I found my answer. God, I decided, had saved me for a purpose. Through my new faith, I would find that purpose.

The Vietnamese government finally relented and allowed me to continue my education, this time in Cuba. It was there that I met my husband—and decided that I would finally escape the clutches of the communist government.

I told no one, just waited my time. And one day, I saw my chance.

It was 1992. My husband and I were returning from our honeymoon in Moscow and the plane needed to refuel in Canada. I looked out the plane window at the wide open spaces of Gander, Newfoundland. We knew nothing of this country except that it was cold—and free. That was enough for me. I had never felt so scared in my life—or so strong. With pounding hearts we left our bags on the plane—and never turned back.

I came here to get away from Vietnam, from the war, and from my life as The Girl in the Picture. I wanted to make my life *quiet*. It did not work out that way, but that's okay. I have found something else—something better. I have found my purpose. I travel and speak out to tell people that war is bad, that tolerance and forgiveness are good, that our real enemy is anger and bitterness.

And I have found that people listen. I believe that's because I speak from my heart. They see me as an innocent little girl who suffered so much, who is supposed to be angry, who is supposed to be dead.

Although I did not become a doctor, I did find another way to heal. In 1997 I established the Kim Foundation, a non-profit group that provides funds for medical assistance to children who are victims of war and terrorism. In 1997, I was appointed a Goodwill Ambassador for Peace for UNESCO.

I could have stayed frozen in time, forever The Girl in the Picture, forever the victim. But I no longer run away, and I am no longer a victim. It was the photograph that saved my life, but it was my reaching out to others that finally convinced me it was a life worth saving.

Chapter 2:

OUR SELF-HELP CULTURE: FOOL'S GOLD

"I never knew how poor I was until I had a little money."[1]
— A banker —

Some 250 years ago, Benjamin Franklin made this observation: "Money never made a man happy yet, nor will it. There is nothing in its nature to produce happiness. The more a man has, the more he wants. Instead of filling a vacuum, it makes one."

"Yeah, right," you may be thinking. "If I had a ton of money, I'd be happy."

We've discovered that this is not necessarily the case. We have met many wealthy people who seem anything but happy.

A few years ago, we attended the World Economic Forum, an annual gathering of business tycoons and economic leaders. We were invited to participate in the Forum as "Global Leaders of Tomorrow" because of our work with Free the Children.

Each year the conference is held in the small but strikingly beautiful ski town of Davos, Switzerland. Its small size makes security more manageable for this elite gathering. Swiss police stand on guard with submachine guns in their hands, watching as invited guests pass through metal detectors. Invitations are extended to presidents and prime ministers of nations and CEOs of the world's largest corporations. Champagne and caviar are served; multi-billion-dollar deals are struck. One night at dinner, a guest joked that if an avalanche ever hit the conference center, a third of the world's wealth would be wiped out. Everyone had a good laugh, except us. We thought it was a rather frightening statement. There they were, just a few hundred people in a room, and a third of the world's wealth was in their control.

On the final day, the conference organizers urged guests to enjoy some of the world's best skiing before leaving Davos. For days, conference-goers had been thoroughly tied up in meetings, attending to the business of signing contracts to generate even more wealth. When the two of us hit the slopes, however, we were surprised to see them virtually empty. The resort's staff told us the lifts were seldom busy during the Forum because the power brokers rarely take the time to ski or even explore the beautiful town—they are all too busy. Despite their wealth, they cannot afford to spend a day at one of the most magnificent winter resorts in the world.

THE ENDLESS CONVEYOR BELT

Since Marc completed his studies at Harvard and Oxford, he has watched a number of his fellow graduates land high-powered, high-paying jobs on Wall Street with investment banks and consulting companies. Others took on positions as lawyers in well-known law firms or as executives at major corporations. As they left student life behind, many of them said goodbye to the roommate with whom they had shared a small apartment for four years, and moved into the new condo that they decorated all on their own. Many had one last drink in the cheap but friendly student hangout and moved on to become regulars at the upscale places that had once been reserved only for birthdays or Valentine's Day. Many upgraded from their old but beloved little matchbox on wheels to a sleek new sports car with tinted windows and a spoiler.

In spite of their apparent success, however, a number of Marc's friends have confided to him that they are not happy. They detest backbiting co-workers and lament 80-hour work-weeks that are expected as "the norm." Some are slaving away for companies that they don't even respect because they pollute the environment or exploit their workers. They often tell Marc how "lucky" he is and how they wish they could follow the same kind of path. But the idea of leaving their jobs to work for something they believe in or finding a position that would give them more time with their families always makes them arrive at the same conclusion: "It's impossible." There are student loans to pay off, the mortgage to think about, and a worry-free, comfortable retirement to secure, starting right now.

Above all, there is a new lifestyle to uphold. Allowing them-selves to slip down the ladder would destroy the illusion of success. How can you walk into the old drinking hole in a three-piece suit carrying a briefcase? How do you park a rusty old beat-up car next to your co-worker's BMW? Things that were once considered luxuries very quickly became necessities.

As more and more people become trapped in this cycle, our opportunities for leisure time often slip away, shifting focus instead to a higher *material* standard of living. The more money we have, the more we spend. We become stuck on an endless conveyor belt, where our consumer appetites continu-ally rise to match our income—so that getting richer does not necessarily make us happier. We want the next upgrade. Often, our satisfaction doesn't depend on what we have, but on how it compares with what other people have, our friends, our neighbors, our colleagues. No matter how much we possess, it will never be enough if the guy or girl next door has more.[2]

The truth is that millions of people never achieve the mate-rial level of "success" extolled in our self-help culture, and the gap continues to grow between the rich and poor. But even those who do "succeed" in a financial sense find themselves stuck in a pathological loop of seeking more and more, and jeopardizing their health and happiness to be able to afford it. The race for more has made American citizens among the most overworked people in the industrial world, putting in, on average, 350 hours (nine workweeks) more on the job each year than their European counterparts.[3]

We are literally working ourselves to death to attain and maintain our cherished material symbols of success. An estimated 43 million people in the United States have high blood pressure, an ailment that is associated with unhealthy living and stress.[4] Heart disease and gastric problems are on the rise as millions drive themselves ever harder in the workplace. Studies also reveal a sleep deficit among working Americans, many of whom sleep between 60 and 90 minutes less than the amount they need for healthy living.[5] Although, as the 1997 National Survey of the Changing Workforce reveals, nearly two-thirds of employees were working more than they wanted to, they continue to be drawn into what former Harvard economist Juliet Schor calls "the insidious cycle of work-and-spend."[6]

We won't lie to you and say that financial freedom would not make a difference to parents struggling to make ends meet or assist the high school grad desperate to find that first job. We are also not saying that you shouldn't buy things, take a vacation, or go out for a nice meal. Money should give us the freedom to enjoy all these things, but it should not be an end in itself. When, in the pursuit of greater wealth, increasingly people find themselves sacrificing the things in life that really matter—friends and loved ones, leisure time, and even their own health. Something is wrong with the notion that money equals happiness. Still, there are plenty of people seeking the material path to satisfaction, convinced that the store-bought brands of "happiness" and "success" will fulfill their promises.

EMPTY PROMISES

Tune into any type of media, from television to radio to magazines to billboards, and we find that we're bombarded with advertisements pushing products that will allegedly make us happy. We aren't told to buy a soft drink because it tastes good, but because it's a window into another life, a better life. Buying a face wash won't only clear our complexion, it will also improve our social life and our chances for love. According to Jessica Williams, a BBC journalist and author, "Branding hopes to sell a feeling, perhaps a whole lifestyle ... If you're not sure where your life is taking you or what you should be trying to achieve, brands are there to help guide you."[7] The success of this strategy is apparent; Williams reports that in a recent survey of 7,000 people in the U.S., Britain, India, Germany, Japan, and Australia, 88 percent of those polled recognized MacDonald's Golden Arches and the Shell oil logo.[8] In 2002, global spending on advertising reached $446 billion, nine times the amount spent in 1950. More than half of that is spent in U.S. markets[9] (that's $2,190 a year per household[10]) and it's working.

The average American spends one year of his or her life watching television commercials.[11] We tune in to these ads in search of much more than a sales pitch; many of us look to them to find our self-worth. "Our entire economy is built on human weaknesses, on bad habits and insecurities," writes humorist Will Ferguson. "Fashion. Fast foods. Sports cars. Techno-gadgets... Diet centers. Hair transplants for men... Our entire way of life is built on self-doubt and dissatisfaction. Think what would happen if people were ever really, truly happy. Truly satisfied with their lives."[12]

More and more, we fill our homes and our lives with objects that give us a few minutes of pleasure and then poof! The euphoric cloud of newness wears off before the "new car smell" does. Studies have described the "surge of pleasure" that people experience after a new purchase, and how short-lived it is, as they quickly adapt to the change.[13] This is not unlike children who tell their parents that they must have the latest toy to be really happy, and within a few weeks are begging their parents for the next toy on the shelf to feel another rush of joy. Psychologist Richard Ryan states that, "satisfaction and dissatisfaction are relative to our recent experience." This helps to explain why "material wants are insatiable" for many people who rely on them for happiness.[14]

Today, Americans spend more money on shoes, jewelry, and watches ($80 billion) than they do on higher education ($65 billion).[15] And by the year 2000, the United States had twice as many shopping malls as high schools.[16] Prioritizing luxury items over education doesn't seem to serve the purpose of self-improvement. More importantly, when approximately 90 percent of teenage American girls report "store-hopping" as their favorite activity,[17] it's clear that these new priorities are a legacy we are passing on to our children. More and more, the shopping center is emerging as the new symbol of our cultural values.

Surveys show that 70 percent of Americans visit malls each week,[18] while, comparatively, weekly church attendance in the United States has declined to 40 percent.[19] Today, "our equivalent to Gothic Cathedrals are the megamalls," note the authors of *Affluenza: The All-Consuming Epidemic*[20]. If this is true, then the greatest of them all is the Mall of America.

"By the time Ray Charles belted out 'America the Beautiful' on the eve of its 1992 grand opening, the Mall of America had already sent shock waves through the Twin Cities," writes Eric Wieffering of the *Star Tribune*.[21] The project's original developers planned to build more than a mere shopping center in Bloomington, Minnesota; they set out to create "the ninth wonder of the world."[22] At 4.2 million square feet, the Mall of America became the largest retail and entertainment complex in the United States. It boasts more than 40 million visitors each year and is promoted as the nation's number one visited attraction, surpassing Graceland, the Grand Canyon, and Disney World combined. "[It] has become a destination for everything from family vacations, weekend getaways and even honeymoons... Once known mainly as a vacation destination for outdoor activities, tourists now flock to the state for *shopping*."[23] The Mall of America has taken on symbolic stature in the Twin Cities, and also, it seems, on a nationwide level. But what does such a monument stand for? What values does it represent? And which ones has it replaced?

THE MEASURE OF HAPPINESS

It seems that once North Americans reach a certain level of financial security, going higher on the financial ladder has very little relation to one's state of happiness. Jean Chatzky, a financial editor for the *Today* show and a columnist for *Money Magazine*, polled 1,500 Americans in 2003, with the help of the Roper Organization, to determine the impact of money on personal happiness.[24] She concluded that more often than not, unless you are desperately poor, and do not have the basic necessities for comfort, money has little bearing on how happy you are. For example, 74 percent of those earning less than $25,000 a year reported overall they were somewhat or very happy with their lives. Among those with a household income of $50,000 only 10 percent more said they were happy. From this point there was "no discernible difference in overall happiness with friendships, standard of living, marriage, children, and appearance," with further increases in income to $100,000 and over.[25] In addition, she found that "people who believe that money equals happiness are less satisfied with their self-esteem, their friendships, and their life overall. A greater number of them worry about their lifestyles, their jobs, and their financial situation. And half of them feel they don't measure up financially to others their age."[26]

The World Values Survey, an assessment of life satisfaction conducted in more than 65 countries between 1990 and 2000, found that the correlation between income and happiness rose at similar rates until about $13,000 of annual income per person. After that point, having more money appeared to yield little growth in self-reported happiness.[27] In fact, the survey revealed that Nigerians saw themselves as the happiest nation in the world, followed by Mexicans and Venezuelans, with Americans ranking 16th.[28] The number of "very happy" people in the United States peaked in 1957. Even though Americans consume twice as much as they did in the 1950s, they were apparently just as happy when they had less.[29]

Our argument here, however, is not that everyone who is wealthy is unhappy. Studies have shown that it is not affluence itself that leads to an unsatisfying life, but rather "living a life where that's your focus."[30] Some CEOs or celebrities we've met have found a great deal of contentment and enjoyment in their lives. The difference is, in our opinion, because they don't see money as their end goal and they do not allow it to control their lives. People like actor and philanthropist, Paul Newman, The Body Shop founder, Anita Roddick, and entertainers and activists like Bono, Peter Gabriel, and Jewel are just a few examples of people who love what they do, are proud of and grateful for what they have achieved, and find happiness in being able to share their good fortune with others.

We have had the privilege of working with Oprah Winfrey's Angel Network on a number of education projects around the world. On an international scale, we have seen how Oprah uses her status, media access, and financial assets to awaken in the general public awareness of pressing social issues and how people can respond. According to Oprah, her outreach to others brings her great personal satisfaction and fulfillment. However, people like her and a few others in this respect seem to be the exception to the rule.

RIDING THE SHOPPING CART DOWN THE ROAD TO NOWHERE

It has been said that a path with no obstacles probably doesn't lead anywhere. Deep down, most of us know that success and happiness are not found simply through the attainment of material possessions. Much of our self-help culture, however, continues to promote consumerism as the ultimate objective to which we should dedicate our lives. And so we spend and consume, pushing ever harder until we can buy that next item on our list, to validate how "successful" and "happy" we are. Often, we actually *prevent* our happiness by pursuing a quest that is, by design, never satisfied, and we lose sight of those things in our lives that are far more important. Once we reach the peak of material success, we open up our prize and find it empty: the big-screen television is just a glass and plastic box; the fancy car becomes just a way to get around; and the big house is just a building that will never be as appealing as the one next door.

My Story

KEITH TAYLOR

For as long as I can remember, I had three dreams. One of them was to become a teacher. One was to live in New York City. And one was to become a philanthropist.

After 14 years of school and about $100,000 in student loans, I had managed to fulfill one of those dreams. I had become a professor. At 32, Ph.D. in hand, I secured the academic Holy Grail—a tenure-track job, teaching in my field, at a terrific university just outside of Nashville, Tennessee. Along the way, I had got married and divorced. I'd become the father of a remarkable little boy. I'd made a lot of good friends.

Still, no matter what I did, no matter how hard I worked, I couldn't make ends meet. My starting salary was barely enough to pay rent, child support, basic utilities, and my student loans. With each little increase in salary came an increase in expenses.

I still wanted very badly to be a philanthropist, but that dream seemed unattainable. To my mind, a philanthropist was someone with hundreds of millions of dollars to funnel into medical research or to build hospitals. I, on the other hand, could barely take care of *myself*. Just when I was ahead on my bills, something else would happen—my car would break down, for example—and I'd find myself behind again.

I still wanted to help people, but I couldn't understand how. That $5 I might give to charity meant $5 worth of gas I couldn't purchase.

So this is how I lived, month after month, for two years. And every month, my dream of becoming a philanthropist seemed farther and farther out of reach until one evening in March 2002.

It occurred to me that throughout my life, there had been many times that people had pulled me through a tough time. They hadn't showered me with thousands of dollars, but rather with tens or twenties to help me with small, unexpected expenses. My father had stepped in to repair my car when he knew I couldn't afford it. My boss had helped me to buy a pair of glasses to replace the ones I had broken while working with him. My best friend in college once paid my power bill when I had been forced to choose between books for class and the light to read by.

None of these people had been rich. None of them had given me very much money and yet their small, one-time gifts had come at just the right time. And they had done this—often giving up something themselves in the process—simply because they cared.

The longer I thought about it, the more I realized that these acts were the very definition of philanthropy. Philanthropy has nothing to do with the *amount* of money. Philanthropy is simply reaching out to help, in whatever way we can, without expecting anything in return.

That's it, I told myself, *no more excuses.* No more waiting until I was "back on my feet." No more waiting to hit the lottery. If I was ever going to become a philanthropist, the time was now.

I began by downsizing my life. I gave up the period apartment I loved and moved into a triplex down the street—a dump at half the price. I got rid of all the "stuff" I'd accumulated over the years, whittled things down to my TV, couch, bed, and dishes. I worked out a new monthly budget. I now had $350 a month—about 10 percent of my income—that I could use to help others.

But how?

In order to find people who needed the kind of help I could offer, I put together a simple website, which I called Modest Needs. I launched that website with a pledge: I promised that every month until I died or the Internet became obsolete, I would use that site to offer 10 percent of my monthly income–$350 a month–to people who didn't qualify for conventional charity (just like me), who were working as hard as they could (just like I was), and who encountered a small, unexpected expense that threatened his or her financial stability (just as I had many times in the past).

The first person Modest Needs helped was a man living in the midwest United States who couldn't pay his car insurance. I asked him to send me his bill, and I wrote a personal check to the insurance company for $78. Putting that check in the mail gave me a feeling unlike anything I'd ever experienced. For the first time in years, I'd done something completely unselfish, and nothing–nothing I could buy or own or have–felt as good to me as that did.

I expected Modest Needs to sit quietly in a corner of the Internet that few people ever visited. I expected to hear from five or six people a month. It didn't matter that I couldn't help them all. I figured if I managed to help just one person a month, then that was one person whose life was a bit better off.

But things didn't go quite as I'd expected.

A few weeks later, on April 1, a friend posted a link to Modest Needs on a community web log. The next morning, I was inundated. About 10 percent of the people who e-mailed me thought Modest Needs was an April Fool's joke. Another 10 percent asked for some kind of help. The rest wanted to know how they could help.

Things snowballed after that. I was flown to New York to appear on the *Today* show and on CNN'S *Morning Edition*. When I returned home that evening, it took me over three hours to download my e-mails.

At that moment I knew my life was never going to be the same.

People often ask me to tell them my favorite Modest Needs story. Without question, it is the mother from Kentucky who needed help for her five-year-old son. The little boy was born with Irlen's Syndrome. His eyes were unable to process shapes, so everything was a colored blur. Lenses to correct this disorder cost $500, plus the frames—which the mother couldn't afford. She told Modest Needs that her son was about to start kindergarten and if we would send her $50 for a down payment, she'd get a second job to pay the rest.

Modest Needs was able to fund the entire cost of the special lenses. Later, I learned that when he was being fitted with these lenses, he looked in the mother's direction, pointed, and said, "Is that mommy?"

It was the first time he had seen his mother's face.

Today, Modest Needs has become more than a non-profit organization. It is a community of philanthropists, exceptionally caring people who have chosen to give up a small indulgence—a cappuccino on their way to work, a hamburger, or a couple of movie tickets—in order to help others. They make this sacrifice not because they have to, not because they feel guilty, but because the pleasure it gives them far outweighs that small indulgence.

Today, Modest Needs helps an average of one person a day, with donations that may be as small as four quarters anonymously taped to a postcard. Since that fateful March in 2002 we've given away nearly a quarter of a million dollars. I don't feel like a knight in shining armor, and I sure don't look like one—more like Jerry Seinfeld, I'm told. But I do feel good. My blood pressure and cholesterol are down, I lost 50 pounds, quit smoking, and even enjoy working out. (I used to think there was no point in running unless you were being chased!) And I've met some amazing people; one even helped me find a beautiful, inexpensive period apartment in my dream town—New York City.

So, in the end, I have attained all three dreams.

Such is the power that we have when we act on the most human of desires–the desire to reach out to others.

Such is the power of philanthropy.

Chapter 3:

OUR SELF-HELP CULTURE: HAPPINESS IN A BUBBLE

"Real happiness is cheap enough, yet how dearly
we pay for its counterfeit."
− Hosa Ballou −
(1771−1852)
Minister, Educator

For the next few moments, let's pretend that our friend−we can call him Bill−has attained the level of "success" and "happiness" promoted by the self-help culture. Bill lives in a home worthy of the covers of *Architectural Digest, Fine Furnishings International,* and *Martha Stewart Living*−he is the envy of all his family and friends but not his neighbors, who live in homes that look the same. Three cars are parked in his garage: the classic BMW he drives to work on weekdays, the SUV he takes away on weekends, and the new silver sports car he bought to mark his birthday (and to fill that annoying third space in the garage). On the walls of his den hang pictures of his ski chalet in Whistler and the luxury condo on Miami Beach.

Each morning Bill wakes up ready to seize the day. He's got time enough to shower before launching into a series of calming breathing exercises and slipping into a crisp designer suit. He runs downstairs and grabs his breakfast-to-go bar. Before leaving the house, he pauses for a moment to regret that he has yet to sit down in his brand-new living room furniture, but realizes that doing so could cause some imbalance to the way the taupe designer pillows sit on the sofa. "Boy, does it look good!" he says to himself.

Driving out of the neighborhood, he slows down to wave hello to the security guard standing at the entrance to the gated community he calls home. The guard greets Bill by name, and Bill would return the gesture, but he has forgotten his name–again. He bows his head and speeds away.

On the drive in to work, a car in front cuts Bill off, and he hits the horn in frustration. The other driver responds to the angry sound with a wave of just one finger. Bill counts to ten and decides to put his anger into its "safe spot" for later. He pulls into the parking lot and notices yet another new parking attendant to greet him–the other three that were new this month have already quit because it's hard to support a family on minimum wage. They should have paid closer attention in high school, Bill thinks to himself.

The one guy who never leaves is the homeless man who has taken up residence in the bus shelter in front of Bill's office building. As always, this fellow has a hand out, mumbling something about spare change and a cup of coffee. Bill takes an interest in the tall city buildings and pretends not to see or hear him. The man holds the door for Bill and says, "How about a smile, friend?" There's no way to avoid him, but Bill doesn't have to worry; as long as he just doesn't make eye contact everything will be okay. He should have *gone* to high school, Bill thinks to himself.

As Bill hurries through the open door, he feels a brief twinge of sadness for the man, then quickly tenses up again and refocuses on reviewing the day's agenda. He has to be sharp because the co-workers upstairs are gunning for his corner office, he has four meetings before 10:30, and he is double-booked for lunch.

As he enters the office, his secretary charges up to him with a stack of urgent messages from irate clients, several co-workers frantically ask him if he has seen page three of the newspaper, and his e-mail in-box has reached its limit. As he crashes down onto the leather chair that has five massage settings and glances around at the framed posters adorning his office walls with picturesque scenes and single words like "leadership," "perfection," "success," and "happiness," his pager, cellphone, and PalmPilot all ring simultaneously with that annoying tone he keeps meaning to change. For a fleeting moment, Bill begins to wonder if there is a job opening in the parking attendant's spot.

Like Bill, many people have become so caught up in the artificial bubble of happiness touted by many in our self-help culture that they increasingly cut themselves off from others. They try to draw inspiration from the things they own, and not from the people they know. They build walls around themselves in order to advance individually without considering those around them. But this way of living is flawed because in our daily lives we come into contact with more people than "me", "myself" and "I".

If you think about it, "self-help" is a rather imbalanced concept. Normally, when we think of the word "help," we think of *other* people. Today, the term "self-help" implies that *only* you can help you: improving *only* yourself, and relying on *only* yourself to solve your problems. So we spend a lifetime taking care of ourselves and trying to reach the goals we are told will equate with success. Too often these goals leave little room for community or helping anyone else.

THE RISE OF INDIVIDUALISM

In a critically acclaimed book, *Bowling Alone: The Collapse and Revival of American Community*, Harvard professor Robert Putnam helps to explain this phenomenon of withdrawal from community as both the cause and result of a larger societal change. Americans, he argues, have become much more isolated; civic engagement, group activities, and volunteerism are on the decline. Since the mid-1960s, the University of California at Los Angeles has conducted annual surveys among first-year college students from across the United States to determine their values and priorities. Those surveyed in the mid-1960s showed a much greater interest in civic engagement than money. By the turn of the century, however, these priorities had been reversed. While three-quarters of the group surveyed said that being "very well-off financially" was a "very important" personal goal, fewer than one-third rated as "very important" such civic-oriented activities as keeping up with politics, community involvement, or protecting the environment.[1]

Now, more than ever, we are a society on the move, changing addresses as frequently as we change cars. At a moment's notice, we are transferable, family and all, to another corporate office in another city. Nearly one in five Americans moves each year and, having relocated, is likely to do so again. We have become accustomed to settling quickly into new environments. New arrivals to the community, however, are less likely to vote, to build friendships and ties with neighbors, or to join civic organizations. Since the mid-1970s, the number of times per year that Americans entertain friends at home has dropped by 45 percent.[2] As Putnam explains, "For people as for plants, frequent repotting disrupts root systems."[3]

As North America sprawls out into the suburbs, we are losing our familiar community meeting ground and increasing the amount of time we spend commuting, by ourselves, in our cars. It's estimated that every ten minutes of commuting time cuts all forms of civic engagement by 10 percent.[4]

Often we feel lost in the mega-malls that have sprouted up across the country; we can't find people we know among the crowds. These mass commercial spaces are not designed to connect us with others, but to move us from store to store, "in the presence of others, but not in their company."[5] Today, it would even be risky for "Ma and Pa" to contemplate starting a small local business. They would pretty well be forced to work for a chain where more products are available to more shoppers at less cost. The big-box merchants settle into their efficient, predictable, quantifiable, and controlled corporate slots—but they don't know us anymore, and we don't know them, despite the best efforts of their smiley-face nametags.

It seems that the more efficient we try to make our lives, the less caring we become as a community. E-mail is quick, but lacks the sentimental touch of a handwritten letter. Fast-food restaurants are indeed fast, but they destroy the notion of a family dinner as people head out for a bite at different times or eat in the car on the way back from the drive-thru. Every industry is constantly coming up with more efficient ways to ensure that their millions of customers are served promptly—from automatic banking machines to scan-your-own grocery aisles. These systems are efficient, but efficient for whom? If they are efficient for us as individuals, how is it that the more we develop all these "efficient" modes to improve our lifestyle, the more our lives become busier and busier and the less time we have for family and community? Instead of 9 to 5, many of us are working from 5 in the morning to 9 at night, with an extra shift at a part-time job just to make the rent. What we gain in efficiency, we lose in community. But can we afford to make this sacrifice?[6]

Perhaps the best indicator of this social decline is our unparalleled obsession with the glass and metal box in our family rooms. Roughly 98 percent of American homes have at least one television, and on average, it's on more than seven hours a day. We watch *Friends* instead of having friends. We are glued to the set to watch real people survive, pick a spouse, or redecorate their home. We live vicariously through TV, and it becomes our world. Making TV a priority begins at a young age and affects the strength of family bonds. In one study, when asked to choose between watching TV and spending time with their father, 54 percent of children surveyed between the ages of four and six preferred TV. In later years, the average American youth watches 1,500 hours of television a year and spends only 900 hours in school.[7] More people–millions– watch the Oscars than watch the news, more interested in the glamor and lives of celebrities they'll never know than in the people in their communities. On average, Americans spend only 40 minutes a week playing with their children, and working couples talk with one another only 12 minutes a day.[8]

The true consequence of the overworked, self-focused, materialistically driven society is that we forget what it was that used to hold us together. But it wasn't so long ago that local shops and city markets bustled with trade, churches and temples were full, and social clubs flourished. All of this bonded us together as a community, creating a feeling that we belonged– that we were part of something bigger than just ourselves. Today, loneliness, depression, and suicide are at record high levels. In 2000, there were 1.7 times more suicides than homicides in the United States.[9] Within the next 20 years, according to the World Health Organization's projections, depression will be the second leading cause of disability in the world.[10]

We miss community. We want it. And we're willing to fake it just to get a taste of connectedness to something, anything. We sign up for speed-dating marathons–25 mini-dates in a night to find the perfect match, spending three minutes or less with each person. The connection gets even less personal on the Internet: too busy to meet someone the traditional way (meeting in person and talking)? Logging on to the safety of cyberspace allows us as anonymous souls with silly code names to exchange information, start a relationship, gripe about some injustice, or speak about the most recent episode of our favorite sitcom.

Community is a dynamic and ever-changing phenomenon, and while a return to the social structures of the past is not the solution, we must recognize that as we change with the evolving community—and forget where we come from—certain vital elements of a healthy society are being lost. Due to our self-help culture, we are experiencing what Boston College Professor Charlie Derber calls "a tear in the social fabric."[11]

NO MAN IS AN ISLAND

Dr. Jonathan White, professor of Sociology at Colby College in Maine, believes that the individualistic pursuit in today's society is destroying our potential for community. He argues, "We have become so caught up in the pursuit of our American Dream, a dream steeped in the ideals of material and consumptive success, that we are more and more willing to do whatever it takes to achieve it."[12]

Somewhere along the path, there has been a shift from working hard to a "win-at-all-costs" mentality. At a young age, we learn to become competitors: from our first game of "musical chairs" where we see that there is one less chair than needed for everyone, to our minor league hockey games where angry parents yell at their children to knock the other kid down. Today's educational institutions are designed to foster this competition so it is no surprise that during their college or university days, many students refuse to share their lecture notes because marks are bell-curved, and the failure of one person improves the marks of others. With this kind of background, can we be surprised when life becomes a competition and there is no remorse felt for the "losers" left behind?

In our travels, we have met some exceptional people who have made us rethink the values and trends of our North American lifestyle. One young man prompted us to re-examine our sense of community as reflected through television and American pop culture. We met him while traveling through the Andes Mountains in Ecuador on a visit to one of the primary schools that Free the Children had helped to construct. He was volunteering in a small village in the region. That night, sitting around the fire, we asked him what had brought him to this remote part of the world. He answered that he had been searching for a place where there was no TV.

He told us that he had been a participant on the first-ever show of the phenomenally successful *Survivor* television series. In this program, 16 strangers are stranded in an exotic but isolated location. The group is divided into two tribes that compete against each other every week in staged contests. The losing tribe must vote off a member, until, in the final episode, after the two teams have merged into one, only two contenders remain to vie for a one-million-dollar prize. To win the contest, a tribe must pull together and work as a team. But the all-for-one, one-for-all philosophy quickly falls apart, as members plot against each other to preserve their spot on the show. The competition brings out the worst in the participants. Petty complaints are aired on camera out of earshot of other tribe members. Bold-faced lies are shamelessly told; pacts are made and broken; alliances are betrayed; and teammates are stabbed in the back.

Far from being repulsed, the public ate it up. Ratings went through the roof, spawning all kinds of copycat shows. People loved it because it was "reality" television—they identified with the ruthless competition they witnessed.

The former cast member we met went on to explain that at the end of the show, he returned to the United States to unexpected fame and fortune. A modeling agency quickly signed him on and he received offers to appear in well-paying commercials. He dated one of the other *Survivor* participants and came to be known as "the guy from *Survivor*" everywhere he went.

Gradually, it dawned on him that he had become trapped in *Survivor*—not the role itself, but in the constant rivalry it stood for. He came to the realization that life in the Western world was just as competitive and brutal as it is depicted in the television series. The opportunities that had come his way all had hidden costs. Instead of feeling worry-free, he felt he was back on the island with the people around him jockeying to get a piece of him. Relationships were treated like commodities— opportunities to get ahead of the pack. He could never let down his guard and be himself. Once again he felt that life had become a battle to be the last man voted off.

In the end he chose to vote *himself* off the island. This time, it was the "island" of North America. With a one-way ticket to South America, he spent the better part of a year traveling from one small impoverished village to another. Everything he owned was in one backpack. He was never robbed. He carried no money and, most of the time, no food. He ate and slept when strangers opened their doors and shared their homes with him. Many people asked him what a "gringo" was doing so far from home. What answer could he give? Even he didn't fully understand why he was on the move.

As he accepted the hospitality of some of the poorest people on earth, he was amazed at how they shared even when they had so little themselves. Instead of a race in which he was to get ahead at all costs, he found that what he really needed was a caring community to which he could belong, where people didn't plot to edge him out, but valued and respected what he brought to their lives. As he traveled about the countryside of Ecuador, witnessing the desperate poverty typical of so many rural communities of the country, he found a place to volunteer, working to bring schools and clean water to poor communities. He could now stop walking.

"GLAD THAT'S NOT ME!"— THE BYSTANDER EFFECT

Except for a shrinking circle of family and friends, our self-help culture is causing millions of us to become more and more removed from the people around us. It is luring us into our own individual bubbles. We may not realize the effect of such detachment when all is well in our world, but run across a bumpy patch and we quickly discover the consequences of this isolation.

This feeling of being alone must have characterized the final hours of Catherine (Kitty) Genovese's life. Genovese died steps away from her New York City apartment, the victim of a brutal attack and rape. Her cries of "Oh my God, he stabbed me," and "Please help me! Please help me!" on March 13, 1964, woke up 38 of her neighbors in her high-rise apartment building. Not one came running to her aid—some even watched from their windows as the attacker dragged the young woman into an alleyway—until finally a lone neighbor appeared with a baseball bat and scared the perpetrator away. But even he left Catherine on the pavement, bleeding and dying. When the coast was clear, the murderer returned to finish the job he had started. Appallingly, the police weren't called until the attack was over and Catherine lay dead.[13]

It was a highly publicized event that shocked and horrified the world and sparked intensive research to explain why people don't act when others are in need. An entire body of psychological literature now exists on this subject, called the "bystander effect." The Genovese tragedy offers a classic case study of this phenomenon: who isn't shocked by the turn of events? How could 38 people listen to a dying woman's screams and do nothing?

It seems that little has changed in 40 years; perhaps it's gotten got worse. For example, in March 2004, a bus driver in our hometown, Toronto, was attacked as his eight-year-old son looked on. When he became involved in a dispute with a passenger, the driver pulled the vehicle over to the side of the road and asked the unruly passenger to leave. He was then struck on the head and dragged off the bus and was kicked and punched. Twenty other people were aboard; not one intervened, and all of them left the scene before the police could interview them as witnesses.[14]

Why do some people choose to be bystanders? Psychologists say that uncertainty, the desire to "stay out of other people's business," and/or the assumption that someone else in the crowd will take action, or "must know more" about the situation, all play a key role. Each individual thinks along the same lines and as a result nobody moves to offer help. Amazingly, because of this, the larger the crowd, the less likely someone is to come to a victim's assistance.[15]

Perhaps people choose to be bystanders because they don't want to take on any more responsibility than they already have. Many people are already overwhelmed by the world around them. One study on the bystander effect found that even among a group of Christian theology students there was reluctance to help a stranger. Late for a lecture, they were told they had to give, the students rushed across the campus. On the way, they passed a shabbily dressed man who lay in a doorway moaning. Only 10 percent of the class stopped to help the individual. Ironically, the students were on their way to give a lecture on the biblical parable of the Good Samaritan.[16]

Often, what holds us back from extending that helping hand to someone in need is a fear that we have something to lose. If we give our time, we fall behind in our schedule of duties and tasks. If we give money, we have less to spend on something for ourselves. Giving and helping do entail a certain sacrifice, but what happens when no one, or not enough of us, is prepared to act?

We may subscribe to an individualistic culture, but ironically, this kind of behavior touches us all, and in very negative ways. Many of us in our communities can't walk the streets at night and feel safe. We deal with the psychological impact of knowing that we step on our co-workers on the way to the top. And we face the fundamental truth that if we don't feel a need to intervene to help others, chances are that they won't feel a need to help us. The famous words of German anti-Nazi activist Pastor Martin Niemöller shed light on this very chilling fact:

> First they came for the Jews and I did not speak out–because I was not a Jew. Then they came for the communists and I did not speak out–because I was not a communist. Then they came for the trade unionists and I did not speak out–because I was not a trade unionist. Then they came for me–and by then there was no one left to speak out for me.

My Story

TIM LEFENS

I was never a "kind" person. It wasn't in my nature. Back then I was anything but. Wildly self-centered, I didn't give presents or flatter people, stuff like that, no tenderness. My friends referred to me as ruthless and I guess I was.

I ran around, did all kinds of stuff whether anyone liked it or not, was King of the World.

My abstract paintings were being shown in New York, in solo exhibitions, getting kudos from the critics. I was swaggering with my buddies through lower Manhattan and across northern Italy, climbing trees, surfing monster waves—artists' loft parties, great women, fast motorcycles. Total freedom. Total celebration.

Total self-absorption.

One day a friend asked if I'd show some slides of my artwork at a school for the severely disabled—people who couldn't walk or even talk. What the hell, I thought. Why not?

Had no idea what I was getting into.

It turned out to be more a hospital than a school. And like you, I'm not anxious to go into a hospital no matter what the reason. So when I strode through the automatic doors, down the shiny linoleum halls in my ratty jeans and T-shirt, I was totally blown away. There were all these contorted bodies, arms strapped to wheelchairs or poking out at weird angles, limbs flailing, mouths drooling. Pretty radical stuff.

This was definitely not a world I wanted anything to do with, such suffocating limits, no freedom. In the room where I was to show the slides of my paintings there was a guy sitting in his wheelchair, his brittle underdeveloped body strapped in, head held aloft by a network of stainless steel wires, hands dangling off the end of the armrests, fingers twisted, bent backwards, welded into knots. I didn't know where to look, but before I averted my eyes from fear, the guy caught me with his, his eyes, and held me with them. "I'm in here," they said without words, steely gray, intense, not weak. "Do you see me?"

I felt a bolt of voltage pass from him to me, the charge blowing through my body. There was a person in there! I took a closer look at the other patients who'd been wheeled in to see my art. The woman I'd seen in the hall, appearing brain-dead, staring at the floor, met my gaze with warm brown smiling eyes. They had given up looking to the staff, but a new person, they'd give a shot to see if there would be any recognition. She threw her head back with laughter, seeing both my fear and the fact that I had indeed seen her, seen the light of her life inside. Next to her, a boy with red hair glared at me. His little arms strapped to his chair, the anger sparked from his eyes to the closed windows, to the lap tray in front of him, back to me again, then back out the sealed window to the outdoors. A worshipper of freedom, this tore me up. This little kid was fierce as a wolf I'd seen held in a dog's pen, no thought of surrender.

I see them! I thought. And they see I see them! Getting past their outer appearance they suddenly appear as people full of energy.

The hospital staff bustled about, distant and distracted. I was supposed to talk about my work, so when the first slide went up, I spoke of the power and freedom of pure abstraction, speaking as I would to colleagues, not as to what some would think of as broken kids incapable of sophisticated thought or feeling.

Pushing the shock of the experience even further it was clear they were linking with the images, no doubt about it. My life of total physical freedom, their lives of total physical limitation, maybe, maybe, painting could be a world we could enter together. But how, with no use of their hands, could this ever be?

Back home, I lay my forehead on the kitchen table, my mind lashed by unfamiliar emotions. I was being disassembled, my old arrogance shattered. All my life I'd been seeking that kind of keen energy in other people, most times to be sorely disappointed, and now here it was, in the most unexpected place, the least likely people. It was too brutal, them trapped not just by their bodies but by the people around them, paid to aid them toward freedom.

I became obsessed, thought about it 24–7, stopped working on my own stuff, dropped everything. Finally, after a bunch of sleepless nights, I knew what I had to do. I had to go back, to get that energy out somehow. Maybe they could paint—not with their bodies—but with their minds.

In a first, somewhat primitive technique, they directed their wheelchairs over paint-covered canvas, their wheel-tracks speaking for them as drawing. It was like unleashing a bunch of maniacs—very raw. One of the first artists, one of the rare ones who could speak, shouted "Wow!" as each new painting was revealed. "Wow!"

Her turn. She attacked her canvas, which was taped to the studio floor, jacking hard on the joystick of her electric wheelchair, jetting forward, then back, her head snapping back, then forward. Then, her wheelchair still, she began to revolve in place on the center of her painting, slowly at first, then faster and faster, round and round, faster, faster, faster. "Take me away!" she cried. "Take me away!"

After that, I was hooked. I thought of a better way for them to paint, with a laser attached to a headband. The students simply looked at where they wanted the paint to be placed and a trained studio assistant applied the paint. Every choice was now theirs— every detail, of color blending, application tool, size, and orientation of their canvas. The results were awesome. In no time the art world took notice. They had sellout shows in important galleries in New York City, their work selling for thousands of dollars. We expanded to include other schools. But for me, the best part was still the "outing": the moment when a quadriplegic snapped free of his limits and lost himself in the paint. Sometimes it happened immediately; sometimes I needed to goad them on, whisper a little in their ear: "Come on, get it going. Do it!" Suddenly that trapped spirit was free, expressing itself through the paint in a way that was absolutely coherent, absolutely magical.

And that's how it happened, how a group of "ultimate underdogs" tenderized my heart, how my casual what-the-hell stroll into a strange institution changed my life and led me into one of the most beautiful profound things in the world–the liberation of people who never thought they'd be free.

I have my own physical challenge now. Got diagnosed with something called RP, retinitis pigmentosa. Doctors said I had two to five years of useful vision left. Don't get weepy for me, it's been scary but I can still paint. The thing I want to tell you is how, when I was lowest, way down there, pretty close to giving up, it was the kids and young adults I worked with who lifted me up. As my sight got worse, they managed to ask about it without me having to say a word. When I fessed up, they gathered around, a close little circle, one of them saying quietly, "Maybe we don't have that much time." Then to break the spell of sadness they jumped back into their painting with added gusto, abandon, showing that when things go black you have only two choices: sit back or push on.

I helped them, then they helped me. It was rich, rich, good stuff. Proves it for real, that it's what's inside that counts and that anything is possible, the spirit indestructible. Thanks to this new world I entered and the vital power I'm touched by, it's a much deeper, more enthusiastic life than I could ever have dreamed.

Chapter 4:

ME TO WE (FROM US)

*"The best way to find yourself is to
lose yourself in the service of others."*
– Mahatma Gandhi –
(1869–1948)
Leader, Indian National Movement

We know that money does not buy happiness, but millions still continue to follow the yellow brick road in their quest for unlimited wealth. And we know that isolation breeds unhappiness, but at almost at every level of education, socialization, and the media, we are bombarded with the message that we must fend for ourselves, compete against others, and always look out for "number one." Instead of recognizing that we are all connected to each other, untold millions of us continue to live as though trapped in an episode of *Survivor.*

If we cannot win the game, perhaps we need to change the rules. It's time that the "Me Generation" makes way for the "We Generation"–people who understand that they are part of something larger than themselves. We need a fundamental shift in how we view ourselves and others, and the connections between us. We need a new definition of "self" and "help," one that inspires us to trust again, to be compassionate, and to stand together.

The *Me to We* philosophy is grounded in only *one* habit— *one* step needed to transform our lives for the better. Some may call it a step forward in thinking, charting a new path in the self-help culture, or presenting a fresh and dynamic way of looking at the world. Others might see it as a step backward, a return to the simplest, purest, and most basic impulse of humanity, to reach out to each other for survival. From either perspective, this philosophy presents a change in focus, a shift from the inside out, and the redefinition of meaning, success, happiness, and community.

While some of the self-help books on the market allot a chapter to the importance of reaching out to others, volunteering in the community, or helping a loved one, it is often the last chapter, the final stage in the evolution of the better self. But this model is flawed because many people have a hard time reaching the perceived level of perfection needed to qualify for that final stage. Improving ourselves is not necessarily a prerequisite to reaching out, but rather a result of that experience. The two of us were fortunate to make this discovery at an early age, and it helped to shape our dreams and our lives.

THE BEGINNING: MARC

In Marc's last year of high school, he told our parents that he was bored and didn't want to spend another year in school. Realizing that he was an excellent student, our parents agreed that he could leave school with the understanding that he would take night classes to complete his course requirements to graduate, and that he would do volunteer work during the day. Thus began one of the most important years of personal growth in Marc's life. He decided to tutor at an alternative education program for students who had dropped out of the regular system; students who had been expelled from school, had failing grades, had behavioral problems and had been in trouble with the police, or were simply turned off by society and life. The local school board had set up the program in a shopping mall, because this was where the young people hung out most of the time. After a half-day of class, the arrangement was that the students would work in the mall for the rest of the day. When he first began this volunteer experience, Marc did not realize that he would be the one to receive the best education of all—one that would transform him completely.

We grew up experiencing what many would call a "charmed life"—with wonderful parents, a middle-class home where there was always food on the table, and people who supported and loved us. That year, Marc learned that this scenario is not the reality for many of today's children. As a tutor, he met students like Andrew, who regularly cleaned the vomit off the floor when his alcoholic father came home from the pub. There was Maria, who had been abused by a relative, had been forced to run away to the streets, and was now struggling to put her life back together. Scott, who had been raised by nannies, had the latest designer clothes but hated his parents and the world. Then there was Ramirez, who had escaped with his family from Chile and was desperately trying to make money to give his brothers and sisters a better life. There were others, and each one of them had their own story.

As he worked with these young people, Marc discovered that they liked sports, movies, and dancing—just like him. They had dreams and hopes for the future—just like him. They wanted to be loved and find their purpose in life—just like him. But life had given them difficult obstacles to overcome. Marc asked himself some tough questions that year. Why was he so lucky? Why was life so cruel for others? He felt as if he had won the lottery—the lottery of life. He decided to work hard with these students in order to share with them the many gifts he had been given: his passion for life, his leadership skills, and his confidence in the power and capabilities of young people.

During his university studies, Marc spent another full year volunteering in Thailand and Africa. In the slums of Bangkok, he worked in a hospice for AIDS patients. Filled with a sense of helplessness and grief, he cried the first time he held a dying man in his arms. In Kenya, he discovered not only the beauty of the Masai culture, but also the absolute necessity of taking action to protect the environment.

Now, ten years later, people sometimes ask Marc why he is not working as a lawyer earning a high salary with a major law firm. As a graduate of Harvard, a Rhodes Scholar with a law degree from Oxford, he has been offered lucrative and powerful jobs in the corporate world. Marc knows why he is working with a children's charity and with school boards to set up leadership and volunteer programs for students. He made this choice because he still believes in the power of youth to change their own lives and the lives of others. He does this work because of Andrew, Maria, Scott, and Ramirez and the many other young people, who, ten years ago taught him that when you are given more than others in life, this bounty is not solely yours to keep. It is given to you to share with those who have received less.

THE BEGINNING: CRAIG

For as long as he can remember, Craig has always enjoyed reading the comics. He found many of them to be quite clever and from a very young age he would select his favorite ones from the newspaper and paste them around the house so that our family could have a laugh for the day. One morning, in 1995, when he was 12 years old and was searching for the comics in the *Toronto Star*, he saw the front-page picture of a boy wearing a bright red vest with his fist held high. The headline read, "Battled Child Labor, Boy 12, Murdered." Craig had never heard of child labor and wasn't certain where Pakistan was on the world map, but he was immediately drawn to the story because the boy was the same age as he was at the time. The article told the story of a child sold into slavery at the age of four. Chained to a carpet loom, he spent 12 hours a day tying tiny knots to make carpets. At the age of ten he escaped but was murdered two years later for speaking out against the exploitation of children. Craig was shocked to discover that slavery still existed– especially among children. He went to the library to learn more about this situation and was so upset by the stories of children forced into bonded labor that he knew that he had to do something. He wasn't certain what it would be at this point–but he knew that he had to try. Craig approached his classmates and friends to help and together they founded an organization called Free the Children.

Free the Children became Craig's passion. He read everything he could find on the issue of child labor; he even asked a friend to search the university libraries because so little information was available at the time. He wrote letters to human rights' organizations, worked with his friends to organize a petition to the federal government, and a garage sale to raise money for the cause. His team of friends spoke to students in their school and at other schools. Craig was soon invited to address community and union groups. After eight months and many questions and challenges on the issue, Craig knew that he had to go to South Asia and meet these children. He needed to learn more from the child laborers, themselves, regarding how North American children could best help.

Of course, it was not a simple endeavor to convince our parents to allow him to go on such a journey! He was only 12 years of age and wasn't even permitted to take the subway alone downtown. For weeks, Craig begged them to let him go. He raised more than half of the money for the plane ticket, wrote to international organizations to help with safety precautions, and convinced a 25 year-old university student, who was a friend of the family, to act as his chaperone. Finally, with safety precautions in place, our parents relented and allowed him to embark on a seven-week tour of five South East Asian countries. It was a learning experience that would forever change his life.

Throughout the trip, Craig discovered a depth of poverty that he could never have imagined and met more child laborers than he had ever expected: children working in fireworks' factories who told him about the explosions that had disfigured and killed their friends; children in brick kilns sold into slavery to repay their families' debts, street kids high on glue who lived in fear of gangs beating and robbing them; a twelve year-old girl who had been sold and rescued from a brothel, and who now spent her days breaking bricks. There were so many–so many others, including Muniannal, a pretty little eight year-old girl with a ribbon in her hair, who sat on the floor of a small grubby workshop wearing no shoes and no gloves, separating used syringes with needles for their plastics–syringes that had come from hospitals, the streets and the garbage. All she had was a bucket of dirty water at her side where she dipped her hand when she cut herself. At one point, she even stepped on the needles with her bare feet to get to the other side of her work area. She had never heard of AIDS. The person sitting next to her told Craig that he had to leave. If Muniannal's boss caught her talking to anyone, he would beat her.

Seeing the lives of these children filled Craig with a deep sense of outrage. He was angry at a world of adults that allowed this abuse to continue. Such poverty and injustice had always seemed to belong to another world–a world that only existed on the television screen and in newspapers. But for the first time, he couldn't change the channel or turn the page. These children were not just images. They were *real*, no different than him, his brother, his friends, and his classmates. He couldn't understand how such stark inequality had come to exist. Were children not all equal? Were they not all deserving of the same rights? Did a child's life matter less depending on where he or she was born?

Craig thought about some of his friends at school and how important it was for them to have the newest basketball shoes, or the latest sweatshirt with the right logo. And he thought about his bedroom at home—all the video games, the clothes in his closet, and the pile of toys under his bed. Did he really need all of these things? Why did he have so much while the children he met had so little? Was it fair?"

Although the problems faced by these children seemed overwhelming, they had not lost hope for a better life. They still dreamed of being free and going to school one day. Craig was so inspired by their courage! He knew that there was little he could do, alone, but he promised them that he would take their stories back to North America and to the world and tell everyone who would listen about the rights of children—the right to be protected, the right to be free from abuse, and the right to go to school. He believed that if more people knew about the situation of the children, they would help.

Nine years have passed since Craig's first trip to South Asia. Over the years, he has had the opportunity to share the stories of these and other children he has met during his travels in speeches and presentations to students, educators, religious groups, and business, union and government officials around the world. Craig discovered that most people he met were also concerned about exploitative child labor and children's rights. Knowing that there were others who wanted to help gave them the courage to become involved. Free the Children quickly grew from a handful of children dreaming about changing the world into an international movement—with more than one hundred thousand young people taking action to protect children's rights.

Craig is still passionate about Free the Children because he believes that *all* children, regardless of their place of birth, have basic rights that must be protected by the world community. We are *all* responsible for today's children. Protecting them is a moral test of our humanity.

THE COURAGE OF CHILDREN

In our travels over the years, we have been fortunate to spend time with many extraordinary people, but those who always leave the deepest impression on us are the children.

Nagashir is one child whom we will never forget. We met him in India, when we visited a rehabilitation center for freed child laborers. All the children at the center had been forced into bonded labor and abused by their former masters. All had heartbreaking stories to tell, but Nagashir's was particularly horrific. He couldn't tell us how old he was when he was sold into bondage; he didn't know. He simply put his hand out to show how small he was at the time.

Years ago, a man had come to his desperately poor village with promises of an education and a good job. Like many other children, Nagashir and his younger brother were sent with him and ended up in a factory, working at a loom, tying thousands of tiny knots to make carpets—for 12 hours a day. In exchange for his labor, Nagashir was given a small bowl of rice and watery lentils at the end of each day. When out of exhaustion and hunger he fell behind in his work, he was whipped and beaten.

It was only the hope of protecting his younger brother that gave Nagashir strength. This same feeling drew the other children together as well, and they relied on each other as a family. When the younger children cried out of homesickness, the older ones would comfort and calm them. When one child was sick, his friends would finish the work on his loom so that he wouldn't be beaten.

Sadly, we learned that this wasn't always enough to protect the children. Nagashir showed us the scars that covered his body. His hands were mangled with cuts from the carpet knife. His master, unwilling to lose any productive time, would fill the cuts with gunpowder paste and light them on fire to coagulate the wounds, then send the boy right back to work. Most shocking were the scars on his legs and arms, and against his throat, where he had been branded with hot irons. This had been Nagashir's punishment for helping his younger brother escape from the factory. The lesson was seared into his skin and his soul. Traumatized, he lost the ability to speak; for years he didn't utter a word.

Nagashir was freed from the carpet factory in a midnight raid and was brought to the rehabilitation center. There, the staff worked with him to slowly help him heal physically and emotionally. Weeks after having arrived at the center, he was found sitting in the garden, singing a song quietly to himself—his first words in years.

When we first met Nagashir at the rehabilitation center he was 14 years old. We wondered if he would ever be able to fully recover from such suffering. Four years later, we met him again, and he looked stronger, happier. He told us that he had finally fulfilled his dream of going to primary school. He had also been reunited with his brother and his family but, surprisingly, had decided not to return to his village. He now travels through the rural areas surrounding Delhi, educating people about the dangers of sending their children into child labor. Even after having suffered so much cruelty, Nagashir had found the inner strength to reach out. He explained to us that by sharing his experience and revealing his scars, he is not only helping to prevent other children from facing a similar fate, but also helping himself to heal his deeper wounds. His new mission gives some sort of purpose or reason to the ordeal that he was forced to go through. It salvages something good from all those years, and it gives him reason to hope.

FROM *ME TO WE*

Coming home from South Asia, we found our once-familiar surroundings cast in a completely different light. We came to realize that while many of us are very fortunate in North America, we often choose not to help others in need. We walk past the homeless on our way to work, we brush past the woman who struggles to lift her baby's carriage onto the bus, and we turn away from the colleague who has a problem with a project. We think that helping others will slow us down or take something away from us. For Nagashir, however, helping others is what brings peace to what can be a brutal world. If this boy, who was stripped of his freedom, dignity, and even his speech is able to reach out to others, why aren't we, who face such milder challenges, able to do the same?

What surprised us most in our travels to many poor countries of the developing world was not the misery or the extensive poverty of these regions, but the happiness and the hope that survived despite it. We saw not only scenes of hunger and suffering, but also moments of community, compassion, trust, and laughter. We saw people coming together to protect one another, sharing what little they had, celebrating with a smile, music, or dance the small pleasures that the world allowed them.

Our purpose here is not to glorify poverty. In countries like India, Brazil, Ghana, or Nicaragua, where some say that the poor are an enlightened group, we know from working alongside them that these people are not fond of their condition. Poverty is bitter, destructive, crippling, and brutal. But in rural areas, urban slums, and shantytowns, the poor reach out and help one another, and this spirit of community is the difference between life and death. These people have something valuable to teach us. When we stop competing against each other and start cooperating, we strengthen the community to which each one of us belongs.

Most of us in North America do not have to struggle the way people do in the developing world, and we quickly lose sight of how privileged we are. This loss of perspective frequently leads us to view the small setbacks in our lives as huge catastrophes.

We often catch ourselves complaining that we are "starving," that "there's no food" in a fridge stocked full, or that we "have nothing to wear" when we have lots of clothes in the closet. Students have nervous breakdowns before exams, gripe about having "too much homework," or resent being "forced" to go to school. We get tied in knots over going to the dentist, discovering a pimple, or hitting a poorly timed red light.

There is a problem in how we respond to life when we view our "obstacles" in isolation—they seem colossal on their own; it seems nothing can be done about them, and our lifelong success and happiness hang in the balance.

In parts of Asia or Africa, when it rains, people rush outside and dance. When drought hits the rural areas, the crops will not grow and there is no food. For people living in these areas, rain is life, and they dance out of joy and gratitude. In our society, we run for cover at the first sight of rain. It often takes a miracle to make us realize that we are blessed, to push us beyond our comfort zone so we stand up to give thanks. To truly get us to dance for joy in the streets, we would probably have to win the lottery (or see our favorite team win the Super Bowl). But when we allow ourselves to take notice of others whose struggles are greater than anything we can imagine, our perspective changes. When we hear the stories of people who have suffered brutal abuse, or speak to the homeless person who sits near a heated grate on the street, or listen to those who have never had the right to vote, this casts our own problems in a new light. We become more aware of our blessings and, more importantly, we realize how much we have to share and why it is essential that we do so.

So how do we live a life filled with meaning and purpose? Where do we find true happiness? We find it in the power of "We." Happiness is not a solitary pursuit. It is not just about us. It is about us in relationship with others and the world. The surest way to find real happiness is to cultivate relationships and to reach out to our community—on all levels of our daily existence. Clergyman Scott W. Alexander says it best: "We have the greatest potential to make ourselves happy not by hoarding money, McMansions, Maseratis or the right Merlot even ... we make ourselves happy by actively engaging in life and generously giving ourselves away ... in right relation, depth relation, caring relation with all the life that intricately dances within and around us. It is by giving and engaging and not by focusing on ourselves that we slowly, and miraculously begin to draw near the elusive, mystery of happiness we so seek."[1]

In the choices we make, the way we treat people, and the way we spend our time and resources, moving from Me to We helps to revive such key human values as compassion, equality, and responsibility. It is a litmus test that we can use when confronted with life's decisions: How will the choice I am making in my life affect our family? Our community? Our nation? Our world? We learn that opening ourselves to others does not cause us to lose time, money, or energy, but rather to gain a higher quality of life. The *Me to We* philosophy provides a tangible way of improving our family bonds and communities, and of building a more just society for all people. By coming together, we fulfill both our collective and our personal potential. In short, by helping others, we help ourselves.

We all know that goodwill can have a very powerful effect. The more we share as a society and recognize the common human rights of those less fortunate, the less we need to fear crime and violence caused by disparity. The more we reach out to our community, the stronger our relationships become with our neighbors and our networks of support. The more we show the people in our lives what they mean to us, even in little ways like leaving a note for a loved one, the more connected and loved we feel in return. Even in the simplest of ways, we do benefit from helping others. We are certainly not the first to observe that small actions like holding the door open for an elderly woman, and hearing her say a friendly "Thank you," can cause any of us to feel better in the middle of a crummy day.

No one is ever too old or too young to begin the move from *Me to We*. In the chapters that follow, we will show you how to integrate this philosophy into your family, workplace, community, and faith group, and how to spread its message to create a societal shift, a movement to turn the self-help culture on its head. We will also help you to understand both the deeper-rooted benefits of this way of life and the practical gains that it provides, such as improved health, greater self-esteem, and even more meaningful relationships. We will begin by looking at the roots of self-help, which in its original form nurtured community, true happiness, and success in a spirit of *We*.

In charting our path, the two of us are often inspired by the words that Nagashir sang that day in the courtyard. We don't know where he learned the song. Possibly, it was one that he had heard as a small boy and had kept safely in his memory all those years. We asked Nagashir to share the song with us, and we would like to close this chapter with the words he sang that day—words that we have never forgotten:

> If you want to live, live with a smile,
> live with love, don't cry.
> Don't shed your tears.
> There are storms, there are disasters;
> in life there are ups and downs.
> But don't shed your tears.
>
> Smile—pain is part of life,
> but finally you get joy.
> If you want to live, live with new hopes,
> live with new aspirations.
> Live with love
> Live with a smile.

My Story

We come now to the stories of two people, one a college student in the United States, the other a renowned social leader from South Africa. Although they seem to be living in completely different circumstances, what links their experiences is the power of *Me to We*. Juxtaposed, their stories illustrate the potential of living this philosophy both in our daily lives and on the world stage. Whether it relates to small actions or international decisions, the *Me to We* philosophy has the power to create happiness, and to liberate and change the world. It is a simple, but profound way of life.

ARCHBISHOP DESMOND TUTU

I have come to realize that I am most happy when I have fulfilled the law of my being. I believe that all of us end up discovering that the law of our being is based on the fact that we are not here for ourselves. If you pursue "self-satisfaction," or even if you pursue "success" fiercely, without any regard to others, you may achieve a certain goal, but you will almost certainly not achieve true happiness. Happiness is not when you are there for "number one," but when you are there for others. Leadership and greatness emerge when one is able to follow the Lord's words and to, figuratively perhaps, wash the feet of others.

In my life, the person who most embodied this happiness was my mother. She was not formally educated, but she was a wonderful person in her caring and her eagerness to share. She was a wonderful cook. But she never cooked just enough for her family. She always imagined that there might be somebody who would come to our house and who would need to be fed. I have said to many people that I resemble her physically; she was stumpy and had a large nose. But it has been one of my missions in life also to resemble her in her spirit, in her generosity, and in her concern for others.

I have found that I am most happy when I am responding to God's initiatives; for many years, this was through my work for my country. My role in helping to end the apartheid system of government in South Africa was not anything that I had planned or dreamed about. In many ways, I became a leader by default because the real leaders were not around. I happened to get a job as Dean of Johannesburg's Anglican Cathedral, which gave me a platform, and I said, "I will use this position to articulate the aspirations of our people." Soon, we were engaged in a campaign against an unjust system. We were on a crusade. We were driven by what God wanted, and what He was pushing us to do. And it was here that we found our purpose.

JONATHAN WHITE

Running behind as always, but this time for an important date that I just couldn't be late for! I found myself at a checkout counter behind an elderly woman seemingly in no rush as she paid her groceries. A Ph.D. student with not a lot of money, I had rushed into the grocery store to pick up a bouquet of flowers and a pack of breath mints. I was in a huge rush and thinking of my upcoming evening. I did not want to be late for this date.

We were in Boston, Massachusetts—a place not always known for small conversation between strangers. The woman stopped unloading her basket and looked up at me. She smiled. It was a nice smile—warm, reassuring—and I returned her gift by smiling back.

"Must be a special lady, whoever it is that will be getting those beautiful flowers," she said.

"Yes, as a matter of fact, she is special," I said, and then to my embarrassment, the words kept coming out. "It's only our second date, but somehow I am just having the feeling that she's 'the one' and I've never in my life felt that before." Jokingly, I added, "The only problem is that I can't figure out why she would want to date a guy like me."

"Well, I think she's very lucky to have a boyfriend who brings her such lovely flowers and who is obviously so smitten with her," the woman said. "My husband, God rest his soul, used to bring me flowers every week—even when times were tough and we didn't have much money. Those were incredible days, he was very romantic and—of course—I miss him since he's passed away."

I paid for my flowers as she was gathering her purchased groceries and putting on her coat. There was no doubt in my mind as I walked up to her. I tapped her on the shoulder and said, "You were right, you know. These flowers are indeed for a very special lady." I handed her the bouquet and thanked her for such a nice conversation.

It took her a moment to realize that I was giving her the flowers I had just purchased. "You have a wonderful evening," I said. I left her with a big smile and my heart warmed as I could see her smelling the beautiful bouquet.

I remember being slightly late for my date that night and telling my girlfriend the above story. A couple of years later, when I finally worked up the courage to propose marriage, she told me that this story had helped to seal it for her—that was the night that I won her heart.

Chapter 5:

THE ROOTS OF SELF-HELP

*"The challenge of history is to recover the past
and introduce it to the present."*
- David Thelen -
(b. 1939)
Author

The *Me to We* philosophy allows us to return to the essence of self-help, to find a truth long forgotten by much of the modern self-help industry: that, in its original form, self-help was a positive and uplifting force, one based on striving to reach the height of human potential, spirit, and virtue. It sought to bring out the best in people, not in order to be better *than* others, but to be better *for* others.

In developing this philosophy, we drew inspiration from "the original self-help books": the ancient verses of many spiritual texts, and the works of renowned philosophers and social leaders. These, of course, were not self-help guides as they exist today. These classics provided a set of human principles for uplifting the mind, the body, and the spirit, and for living a pure and fulfilling existence. These are the original writings providing life direction, advice on relationships, and guidance on achieving happiness and purpose. What sets these works apart from those of the modern industry is the essential balance they encouraged between building a meaningful life for oneself, and reaching out to do the same for other people and the community as a whole.

HOLY TEXTS

The two of us grew up in a community of faith, but what we learned as children took on a deeper meaning when we traveled to the remote mountainous communities of Nicaragua and met a priest named Padre Carlos.

Padre Carlos was a dynamic person, brilliant and full of life, with a great sense of humor. He had been educated in Brazil and in Rome and spoke five languages, but he told us that his best education was working with the remarkable people of Waslala, one of the poorest areas of Nicaragua. When Padre Carlos first arrived, the region was emerging from a divisive civil war that had crippled its social, physical, and environmental capacities. There was no running water and no electricity, and he slept on the floor of a small hut. Over time, he worked to develop solidarity and confidence among the people and helped them to bring clean water, education, and health care to their communities, earning him their trust and admiration. We developed a working relationship with him to bring schools and education to the children of the area.

We were overwhelmed by the poverty and very difficult conditions we witnessed in Waslala, and by the large geographical area, accessible only by mule, that Padre Carlos had to cover. We asked him if he ever questioned his faith in the face of all this suffering, knowing that it would not be possible to help everyone. He replied that it was not his role to lift every person out of poverty. As he saw it, his job was to give the poor the means to lift themselves out of the oppression to which they had been subjected for so long. So while he provided people with the seeds and tools, it was up to them to sow them, tend the fields, and feed their families—to help themselves and their community. To illustrate this balance, he shared a story with us.

A man heard that a flood was coming through his town. His neighbor told him to evacuate. He replied, "No, you go. I am a man of faith. God will protect me." As the water began to rise, a man in a boat came by and called to him to get in and flee to safety. "No," he replied, "save someone else. I am a man of faith. God will protect me." The water now reached the eaves of the house, and the man was stranded on his roof.

A police helicopter hovered overhead with a ladder dangling. Over a megaphone, the police called down, telling the man to climb the ladder. This was his last chance for survival; the water was rising too high. Again the man replied, "No, go find someone else. I am a man of faith. God will protect me." Eventually the tide rose farther, washing the man to his death. When he arrived at the gates of heaven, the man demanded that St. Peter give him an audience with God. He asked God: "I had such great faith in you; why didn't you protect me?" God replied, "What do you mean? I did. I sent you a neighbor, a rowboat, and a helicopter."

Padre Carlos told us that the story had a deeper meaning that revealed two important dimensions of his faith. "Christians," he said, "are called to serve and to help others. But at the same time, we must use God's gifts to help ourselves." The biblical stories of Jesus' service to others are almost endless.[1] He performed powerful miracles, brought acceptance and hope to the poor and disenfranchised, and provided guidance and inspiration to countless others. As word about His healing power spread, people who were ill, lame, and blind began to seek Him out in huge numbers. He was so overwhelmed by the crowds that at one point He asked his disciples to take Him away by boat to the other side of the Sea of Galilee so He could rest.[2] The Bible also relates the story of Jesus spending 40 days and 40 nights alone in the desert to cleanse His body and mind and renew His spirit to prepare for the ordeal of His final days on earth.[3]

This balance of helping the self and serving others is also evident in the teachings of Judaism. The *Mishna*, which contains the compilation of Jewish Oral Law along with the commentaries of philosophers and rabbis, clearly outlines the principle: On one hand faith says, "If I am not for myself, who will be for me?" The next line follows, "If I am only for myself, what am I?"[4] The *Torah*, which reveals God's instructions to the Jewish people, clearly mandates responding to the needs of the poor and the infirm, be they Jews, strangers, or even enemies. Doing *tzedakah*, or righteous deeds, is part of one's obligation to help repair the world. Importantly, the highest level of *tzedakah* is assisting a poor person by putting him in the position where he can dispense with other people's aid.[5]

This balance is also found in Islam. One of the pillars of Islam is charity, or *zakat*, which requires Muslims to give away a certain percentage of their belongings to the poor as well as make regular donations to those in need. This act of charity and helping others is a means of purifying one's soul from selfishness. People are called upon to help others, not only on a material level, but also by being a good example, by acting with wisdom and kindness.[6] The *Qur'an* contains many passages that encourage social service: "Have you ever seen a human being who contradicts the essence of faith? That is the person who pushes the orphan aside and does not promote feeding the needy."[7] In Islam, each individual is said to have a purpose in life that is provided by Allah, and this purpose is to strive toward the good. Helping others is believed to yield rewards— for example, the love and care of other people—and Allah's blessing on the Day of Judgment. It leads to a better life and fate for the self.

In fact, this duality of caring for both the self and others is present in virtually all religions, and despite their differences, all come together in one central tenet: *Do unto others as you wish them to do unto you.* The following is a list of world religions and their interpretations of this Ethic of Reciprocity:[8]

- Hinduism: "This is the sum of duty: do not to others what would cause pain if done to you." (Mahabaratha 5:1517)
- Taoism: "Regard your neighbor's gain as your own gain, and your neighbor's loss as your own loss." (T'ai Shang Kan Ying P'ien, 213–218)
- Native spirituality: "We are as much alive as we keep the earth alive." (Chief Dan George)
- Buddhism: "Treat not others in ways that you yourself would find hurtful." (Udana-Varga 5.18)
- Islam: "Not one of you truly believes until you wish for others what you wish for yourself." (The Prophet Muhammad, Hadith)
- Judaism: "What is hateful to you, do not do to your neighbor. This is the whole Torah; all the rest is commentary." (Hillel, Talmud, Shabbat 31a)
- Christianity: "In everything, do to others as you would have them do to you; for this is the law and the prophets." (Jesus, Matthew 7:12)
- Sikhism: "I am a stranger to no one; and no one is a stranger to me. Indeed, I am a friend to all." (Guru Granth Sahib, p. 1299)
- Baha'i Faith: "Lay not on any soul a load that you would not wish to be laid upon you, and desire not for anyone the things you would not desire for yourself." (*Baha'u'liah*, Gleanings)
- Janism: "One should treat all creatures in the world as one would like to be treated." (Mahavira, Sutravitanga)
- Unitarianism: "We affirm and promote respect for the interdependence of all existence of which we are a part." (Unitarian principle)
- Zoroastrianism: "Do not unto others what is injurious to yourself." (Shayast-na-Shayast 13.29)

Nothing captures more fully the essential balance between the individual and the community than this Ethic of Reciprocity, the principle that we should treat others with the same respect and dignity that we seek for ourselves. According to the Dalai Lama, "Every religion emphasizes human improvement, love, respect for others, sharing other people's suffering. On these lines every religion had more or less the same viewpoint and the same goal."[9]

A few years ago, Craig was invited to speak at the International Human Rights Film Festival, hosted jointly in Israeli and Palestinian cities. The trip gave him the opportunity to speak with Israeli, Palestinian, and Bedouin children. The Bedouin population lived in the Negev Desert for hundreds of years prior to the establishment of the State of Israel. These people are characterized by their nomadic and rural lifestyle, and now suffer from a lack of basic infrastructure such as schools, employment opportunities, and health services.

One of Craig's first visits was with a Bedouin community— a barren site of tents and shanty houses, with no electricity or running water. The children explained to Craig that many other people, presidents and important visitors among them, had come to visit their community accompanied by the media and promised to send them computers. But the computers never came. All the children wanted were pencils. Could Craig please send them pencils?

Craig was deeply moved to see the children living in their poor conditions. The following day, he had a workshop with Palestinian and Israeli children organized by local groups working for peace in the area. Before he could begin the session, however, chaos and shouting broke out in the room, as children from both groups angrily focused on their historical divisions. With great difficulty, Craig interrupted them and attempted a highly personal form of peace building.

He spoke in detail and from the heart about his visit the previous day with the Bedouins, describing their abject poverty and their plea for school supplies. Both the Palestinian and the Israeli children were touched by his words. After all, they could relate to the Bedouin youths because they were all around the same ages. The Israeli and Palestinian children agreed to temporarily set aside their differences and spent the rest of the workshop planning how they could work together to help the Bedouins. They decided that with the help offered by Canadian young people, they would gather and distribute school supplies to the children living in the Negev Desert. As the session drew to a close, a sense of goodwill had replaced the hostility of the morning. These Israeli and Palestinian children had discovered common ground with people whom they had always perceived as the "other," or as people to be feared. Coming together to help those in need had given them something to identify with and respect in each other—a purpose that rose above religious and political differences—that was basic to them all as human beings.

The truth is that you don't have to be of a certain faith or, indeed, of any faith at all, to appreciate that helping others is as central to the human experience as helping oneself. This sense of balance is found not only in the religious texts and oral teachings of faith groups, but also in the thoughts and writings of philosophers who have since ancient times contemplated the meaning of life and happiness.

PHILOSOPHERS

Ancient philosophers have long reflected on the need for balance between concern for one's self and for one's community. The Greek philosopher Plato argued that the best life for any individual is that which is devoted to the pursuit of knowledge.[10] This knowledge is not gained in isolation, but instead through simple dialogue, in which we exchange opinions with others. In essence, we are all able to find some share of happiness so long as we are willing to listen to others and to consider their ideas carefully, and then work with them to come up with new, better ideas as to life's purpose and meaning. Aristotle argued in his *Politics* that human beings develop virtue (that is, develop their excellence as human beings) through social interaction. This is not a Western concept, as this balance is found in the Chinese philosophers Lao Tzu and Confucius,[11] and the great Islamic philosopher Al-Farabi.[12]

Perhaps the most "self-help"-oriented system in the world is capitalism, which celebrates competition and the individual pursuit of wealth. The Scottish economist Adam Smith is touted as a father of free-market capitalism, with his seminal work *An Inquiry into the Nature and Causes of the Wealth of Nations*.[13] What is less well known is that Smith wrote his economic work as part of his work as a moral philosopher. Smith also wrote the *Theory of Moral Sentiments*, in which he suggested that human beings tend to be self-interested, but they benefit from cooperative interaction to secure their individual and collective well-being. These two seeming extremes–free market competition and moral cooperation–actually go together.[14] Smith argued that if we hope to enrich ourselves (economically and morally) we must constantly be aware that we are rooted in communities. Our actions affect others and the actions of others affect us.

SELF-HELP TAKES SHAPE

Benjamin Franklin, who helped draft the American Declaration of Independence, was a philosopher, printer, social engineer, and statesman. Author of the phrase "If you would not be forgotten, as soon as you are dead and rotten, either write things worth reading, or do things worth the writing,"[15] Franklin did both. His classic 1790 autobiography is hailed as one of the greatest self-help classics.

Franklin was the original self-made man, but he was not only concerned with improving his own life. In a second book, *The Art of Virtue*, he summed up his life philosophy by listing 13 qualities that one should aim to possess. His list reveals a fine balance, evident throughout his teachings, between self-development and service to others. During his lifetime, Franklin helped to establish and refine institutions such as circulating libraries, public hospitals, mutual insurance companies, agricultural colleges, and intellectual societies. In an age when a single fire could consume whole neighborhoods, Franklin founded Philadelphia's voluntary firefighting club, called the Union Fire Company, in 1736. Only seven cloth bags and two buckets were required for membership. Franklin demonstrated that helping others was an act of true patriotism, necessary for the success of the community and each individual.

Although Franklin gave us the essence of the self-improvement philosophy, it was Samuel Smiles, author of the 1859 classic, *Self-Help*, who gave us the term "self-help." No, the book was not about positive thinking, and yes, "Smiles" was actually his real name. In many Victorian households, this book took on a status second only to the Bible. In it, Smiles evaluated historical figures from Sir Isaac Newton to Michelangelo, as well as his own contemporaries, and concluded that the key to success was not talent, but hard work. "Character is power, more than knowledge is power," he concluded.[16] He claimed that our personal success depends on how we relate to others. Trust is the glue that holds free societies together, he argued, and success would belong to those who could be trusted, those who maintained their integrity.[17]

The 20th-century psychologist Abraham Maslow also examined the qualities of human greatness and success, but introduced a psychological approach. He studied the lives of people like Abraham Lincoln, Albert Einstein, Eleanor

Roosevelt, Frederick Douglass, and Albert Schweitzer—all of whom he considered to be "self-actualized," namely, living and contributing to society to their fullest potential.

The core of Maslow's theory is that human behavior is shaped by a hierarchy of needs; from survival needs (food, air, and water), to safety and security needs, followed by love, belonging, and finally self-actualization at the top. This hierarchy is often misunderstood to indicate that people must turn inwards and focus solely on themselves before they can be "self-actualized" and able to help others.[18] Yet community is required to fulfill many of the basic needs, such as security, love, and belonging. And when we examine the lives of self-actualized people whom Maslow used in his study we discover that the subjects were some of the most giving people in history. It was through their concern for others and the actions they took to help humanity that these individuals became great people. Maslow's model reveals that all possibility for human development and fulfillment rests upon moving from *Me* to *We*. If we don't look out for others and have others look out for us, we will be unable to pursue our lives to the fullest.

HISTORIC SELF-HELP GROUPS

We recently traveled to Sierra Leone in West Africa, an extremely poor nation torn apart by a bloody and destructive civil war over the control of the diamond trade. Ever since a fragile peace accord was signed, United Nations troops and other volunteer agencies have been helping to restore order, and for our part, Free the Children has been actively building schools in the country.

Among those most severely affected by the war were the children of Sierra Leone. Some as young as eight or nine years of age were forced to fight as soldiers. These children now suffer severe emotional and psychological trauma and are often outcasts from their communities because of the violent acts they committed during the war against their own families and neighbors. A number of international organizations have been working to help these children deal with their grief and reintegrate them into their communities. We met with one of these groups in the capital city, Freetown, and were invited to join a healing circle that had convened in a local schoolroom. When the meeting began, participants were encouraged to share their thoughts and experiences with the group. A young boy came forward and introduced himself, using only his first name. The group welcomed him, and he began to share his story about the horrific things he had been forced to do as a soldier, and the overwhelming guilt and anguish he now felt. The group listened quietly, nodding, crying with him at times, and whispering comforting words of support and encouragement. We later asked the social workers how they had developed the program for treating these children. They told us it was based on the mutual support model used by Alcoholics Anonymous.

Alcoholics Anonymous (AA) was founded in the 1930s as a network to help recovering alcoholics deal with their addictions. AA is sometimes described as a community of strangers bonded by a common pledge.[19] "Unity, fellowship, and service are the three legacies of AA," remarked a public information coordinator for AA in Toronto. As individuals join a group and attend meetings, sharing their experiences with people who understand, they develop a sense of commitment and responsibility toward other members. Every person has a sponsor whom they can call upon when they feel the urge to drink and need support. This is a mutually beneficial relationship. "Sponsors also help themselves by helping the person they sponsor," the AA spokesperson explained. "They develop their sense of responsibility because someone is counting on them, and it helps them keep their sobriety."

It is not only during the lowest moments of personal crisis, such as a struggle with alcoholism or drug abuse, that we can seek support and friendship built on the values of "unity, fellowship, and service." In our daily lives, we often have the opportunity to reach out to other people—to create a shared existence and experience the happiness, well-being, and energy that this brings. As the teachings of religious texts, philosophers, and social leaders remind us, opening our lives to others is not only essential to our personal and social harmony, it is also the key to reaching the height of our human potential.

Imagine having a connection with others that makes us stronger as individuals and as a collective. Imagine a world in which we all have a community to lean on—one in which we can each feel the tremendous sense of empowerment and boost in self-esteem from being that community for someone else. Imagine a world with *We* at its core!

This kind of community is closer than we think.

My Story

RICHARD GERE

Besides His Holiness the Dalai Lama, my father was and is the most spontaneously generous, responsible, and committed person I've known. I didn't quite understand what that meant when I was a kid, and I certainly didn't understand the special quality of spontaneity that my father embodied. I found it a bit confusing that he would respond to anyone who would call the house with a problem. He was gone a lot doing that. I probably was a bit jealous that he was off helping almost anyone who would call. Later in life I've come to value and understand it more.

When I met His Holiness the Dalai Lama, I had been practicing Buddhism for some time. The wisdom aspect of it attracted me enormously: the exploration of the nature of mind and the evaluation of reality, what we take to be reality. But the compassion side of it was something I hadn't worked on very much, although I think I had an instinctive feeling of empathy for other people's suffering and my own. Meeting the Dalai Lama and the Tibetan community and feeling this incredibly textured and deep exploration of the mind, along with their extraordinary ability to explain, communicate, and activate compassion—a sense of deep, emotional, and unmistakable connection with all beings—had an enormous impact on me. It still does.

Very quickly when I began to be a student of His Holiness and other fine Tibetan teachers, I realized that true spiritual work is much more all-inclusive than I had originally thought. It rejects nothing of life. It is beyond any idea of religion, beyond any concepts. It really is universal in the sense of heart and

mind encompassing universal connections, universal responsibility–beginning to have an actual taste of what is called relative
bodhicitta, which we would probably call genuine compassion.
I began to see that nothing I can do will bring me happiness
unless it includes happiness for others. Whenever I suffer, it's
really because I have discounted the other. The flip side of that
is being genuinely concerned for the other. When this happens,
we have a true spontaneous moment of satisfaction, happiness,
and joy. There is no question in my mind that everything of
value that I have done in my life since then has been informed
by at least trying to engage that deep sense of open-hearted
commitment to relieving the suffering of others that I witnessed
in my father and His Holiness the Dalai Lama.

I am continually amazed that the simplest thought, the
simplest action has waves that, when motivated properly, res-
onate with joy and creativity throughout the universe. I see this
when I get a card or a letter or meet someone on the street who
was deeply moved by something that I had been involved in.
We have a photograph here by Nicky Vreeland of a monk from
Rato Monastery. I knew we were helping a lot of people by
starting a health insurance plan in the Tibetan refugee community, but for some reason I never personalized it. Then Nicky
gave me this photograph of this young monk who had not
been able to walk properly his whole life. He was able to have
an operation through the insurance plan that we put together
and he's walking now and able to sit properly in meditation
without pain, and now we have this photograph of this won-
derfully happy, joyous, young monk. I didn't do it specifically
for *him,* but these are the waves that go out. As soon as any
well-motivated thought or action begins, those waves do have
a positive effect on the world.

I think that prayer is a really important part of any worthwhile activity–spending quiet time with oneself, literally

praying, whatever your idea of praying is, but talking to your purest heart. Life for us is a given and we very much exaggerate our place in it, but I think the universe is more or less indifferent as to what our lives mean. It is our job to make life meaningful; no one can do that for us. We start by looking at our own hearts and by sympathetically realizing that all beings are just like us. We all want to experience happiness and avoid suffering. That is true of animals, insects, those we take to be our enemies, and all beings in all universes. From this point of view there's no enemy, there are only brothers and sisters. We also need to realize how a simple thing like walking in a room and thinking, genuinely from the heart, "I wish you happiness" to everyone in a room, how transformative and healing that is, not only for them, but for ourselves

There are a lot of good people doing wonderful things in the world and as soon as you talk to your own heart and genuinely wish to do good, the opportunities arise almost immediately. They don't have to be big. These waves can start quite small but as they go through the universe, they can have an enormous effect. Even stopping ourselves from getting angry in a moment when we normally would have gotten angry without thinking—that moment of catching ourselves and perhaps even turning that into love and patience and compassion—that has an enormous effect on us and everything around us.

In dealing with difficult people, you have to start from a place where you don't have the answers. I think we genuinely have to listen and to see that everyone has a story and a point of view. There are no true monsters; we're all redeemable and we're all in this together. I'm constantly amazed by the number of times that the people I may be diametrically opposed to politically, who seem to have a totally different world view than mine, someone I may even take to be an enemy, how often we end up doing extraordinary things together to help the world. I think you have to be able to quiet yourself a little bit to be able to listen. Then something effective and positive can happen.

Chapter 6:

THE *MINGA* AND COMMUNITY

"In hell, people are given very long chopsticks, longer than their arms, with which to eat. As they pick up food with the chopsticks, turning it toward their mouths, the food remains beyond reach. And although there is an abundance of food, everyone is starving. In heaven, on the other hand, people have the same long chopsticks, but everyone is full and content. The difference between hell and heaven is that in heaven, people don't try to feed themselves with the long chopsticks; they feed each other."

— Japanese fable —

The power of the *Me to We* philosophy is its ability to create or rebuild community, a caring and supportive network of people we can count on no matter what.

The term "rebuild" does not mean to return to the social structures that existed decades or centuries ago, many of which were restrictive and discriminatory and were overcome only after years of struggle. Instead, to "rebuild" means to cultivate again the spirit of community within today's society, allowing people to stay true to their natural human impulse to reach out to one another. This *spirit* isn't only a phenomenon of the past; it is very much alive today, and we have seen it take dynamic and inspiring shapes.

Throughout the world, there are places where a strong sense of community and reciprocity still survive. There are cultures that have not forgotten that in our most natural state—away from cars and one-bedroom condos and the glare of the television screen—human beings are social creatures who need each other to reach their highest potential. Throughout our travels over the years, we have had the opportunity to learn from many of these cultures and peoples, and have seen the practical application of the *Me to We* philosophy in building community.

THE *MINGA*

Through our visits to Ecuador, we came to work with the Puruhae, an indigenous group living in the foothills of the Andes Mountains. Like many indigenous groups around the world, the Puruhae were for decades subjected to a slave-like serfdom on their land. In the 1960s, they finally won their freedom, but all the best land had already been claimed by the hacienda owners, their previous masters. The only farms they could establish were located in Ecuador's rugged highlands, offering poor soil and little agricultural potential. With their remarkable resolve, however, the Puruhae have sustained themselves on this land, surviving the best way they know how: together.

We quickly discovered the Puruhae were a fiercely proud people who would not accept charity. When they asked for help in building a primary school, they pledged their own labor. They insisted on working together with us in solidarity. One of the elders in the community sent word that a *minga* would be held to build the school. On the appointed day, a crowd arrived—elderly men and women, mothers carrying babies on their backs, and young people walking alongside parents. Men left their fields at peak harvest time to come and join the scores of others on the construction site. Hundreds of people came from all over the region to help build the school. The most extraordinary thing about the *minga* was that it drew people from well beyond a single community. Many workers came in from neighboring villages to help with the project, although they would never personally benefit from it because the school would be too far for their children to walk each day.

The elder of the village, a tiny but commanding woman, explained to our translator that a *minga* is "a coming together of community, to work for the betterment of all"—an event in which people work together to accomplish a task that is far beyond the scope of one person. When we asked what moved the people to act in this way, she told us that some things are sacred, and among them are children and education. "Children," she said, "are the future of the villages—of all the Puruhae indigenous people." According to these communities, there is no future in isolation. The future is shared by everyone.

Our translator struggled to explain the concept of the *minga* and asked us what English word is used to describe this type of community event in our country. We stopped, thought for a moment, and then looked at each other. We were dumbfounded. We could not translate this word into English. A "riot" denotes a public act of violence by an unruly mob, but what about a communal act of kindness? The words "charity," "volunteering," and "mission work" all relate to helping the less fortunate, but these words do not denote the significant level of community participation we were witnessing. There used to be "bees" and "barn raisings" in pre-industrial times, but as much as we tried, we simply could not find a modern English word that encapsulated the spirit of cooperation taking place in front of us. As far as we knew, it didn't exist.

It has been said that the Canadian Inuit have anywhere from 10 to 49 different words for snow (depending on our lexicological preferences, which we will thankfully not get into here), and that the Japanese have numerous words for rice. Linguists suggest that language reflects social priorities. When something is particularly important to a culture, people will create more words to describe the variations within the concept. Just think of how many alternatives we have for the term "money": dollar, cash, buck, greenback, moola, dough, etc. But while there may be, in fact, a word in English that denotes the remarkable community participation we saw that day, we have yet to find it. When our culture does not have a word to describe "a coming together of community, to work for the betterment of all," we must ask what that reveals about our social priorities and what kind of change we need to see.

WE ARE SOCIAL CREATURES

Like the Puruhae Indians, there are other groups around the world who have yet to be consumed by the self-help, self-focused culture and who understand that there is a measure of joy and security to be found in working together. The Masai tribe is one such group, and its people have much to teach us about the power of community. They are the guardians of much of the great expanse of land near the Great Rift Valley in Kenya, East Africa, where anthropologists Louis and Mary Leakey famously unearthed fossils of *Homo habilis*–"handy man"–the oldest known primate with human characteristics. No matter how many times we visit this region–the "cradle of humankind"–it is always humbling to stand on this ground.

Once, when we were driving in a remote area of Kenya and got lost (we *always* get lost–there are no road signs in the wilderness), a goat herder offered to accompany us to our destination. He went six hours out of his way to help two strangers. It wasn't the only time we've experienced such generosity: when hiking with the international volunteers who accompany us to the Masai Mara, people in the nearby villages bring us food and water, refusing any payment. Although they have little in the way of material goods, and sometimes almost nothing to eat, the Masai people will go to great lengths to lend a helping hand—occasionally without eating in order to provide a guest with food.

We have been welcomed into villages and been invited to witness elaborate tribal ceremonies with song, dance, and marvelous local fare. The sense of community we felt when 300 Masai gathered to mark an important annual cultural celebration was nothing short of amazing. They were all dressed in their traditional clothing, characterized by elaborate beaded necklaces for the women and bright red garments for the men. At one such gathering, goats were slaughtered in our honor and the first piece of meat was offered to us. The elders invoked the spirits of their ancestors, taking a mouthful of fermented goat's milk and spitting it at our feet. They gave us Masai names, and they explained that by doing so, they would always defend and protect us and that we were now members of their tribe. In this kind-hearted assembly, we felt a bond of community, hospitality, and continuity with the past.

Before beginning our development projects in the Mara, we spent weeks learning about the community and its needs. We sat under a large acacia tree with the intense sun overhead; we discussed for hours how our organization might be of help. Through this process, we built a friendship with the elders. They shared with us stories of the past, helping us to understand a way of life that is becoming increasingly difficult to find in our self-help culture. Originally nomadic by nature, the Masai have always had to depend on each other to survive. Community members suppress their immediate interests for the greater good. In the area in which we work, they herd their cattle together over huge tracts of land to minimize risks and reduce the impact of drought on individual herders. When it comes time to move on from the village and follow a herd to a better feeding ground, everyone's help is needed to pack up.

No single person is left behind because the Masai people recognize that no individual can survive alone in this harsh land. The Masai believe that the only way they can move forward is by working collectively as one.

COMMUNITY: "AN ANIMAL INSTINCT"

One morning, after a hot breakfast over an open fire, we were chatting with one of our *askaris* (Swahili for guard), whose job was to protect us from the very creatures we had come to see in East Africa. On this morning, we were watching a herd of zebra grazing nearby. On the open savanna, the zebra are the easiest animals to spot because their black and white stripes stand out against the muted browns, greens, and deep reds of the Kenyan landscape. We wondered if evolution had played a cruel joke on the zebra by making it an easy prey for lions and leopards, which, with their keen eyesight, can spot its stripes miles away. The *askari* laughed. "Imagine you are a lion," he said, leaning in to the fire. "Now look closely and tell me which zebra would you pick to eat?" We looked over at the herd, trying to pick out just one. It was impossible. Their stripes blended into one mass and we could not tell where one zebra began and another ended. The stripes were camouflage, as long as the zebra stayed together. It seems that need to be with others is basic to not only human nature, but also to much of nature itself.

The *askari* explained to us that he used to work with a group of foreign researchers who studied the health and migratory patterns of the zebra. Since they, like us, couldn't tell one from another, it seemed to them that it would make sense to dab a blot of red paint on one of the animals, making it easier to track it in a group. But each zebra they singled out for study rarely survived the ordeal. A few days later it would be tracked and killed by a lion or other predator. By adding just that touch of red paint, the scientists had made it easier for predators to visually separate one zebra from another, disrupting the protective power of the group. The *askari* said the researchers were mystified for weeks as to why their plan was not working, until they finally asked him, and he gave these "experts" the explanation.

The zebra isn't the only animal opting for the social life. As we observed them, it dawned on us that the vast majority of animals roaming the great plains of East Africa have a common characteristic—they are community-oriented social creatures. They travel in herds, hunt in packs, and establish colonies to breed. They have an instinct to band together that goes beyond the bond of parent and offspring. Elephants, for example, when frightened will circle around all the herd's young, creating a protective barrier. Chimpanzees, biologically our closest living ancestor, share joy with each other in a physical manner, patting, kissing, and embracing when they encounter an abundance of food.[1]

THE BUS DRIVER HAS A NAME

Humans are by nature creatures of community. It's in our bones. The first people to walk the earth survived only because they worked together to feed and clothe themselves. This was a community of hunters and gatherers who shared skills and knowledge on what berries were edible, where water was to be found, and how to bring down an animal using only a simple weapon. The fresh meat would be good for only a short time, so they would have to share their catch.

Even as humans settled on the land, sowing crops and raising animals, they had to rely on one another to bring in the harvest, build a church, or raise a barn. Villages and towns sprung up as people traded skills and services for goods. With a more stable food source and fewer natural dangers to face, populations grew. Village life, in which everyone knew one another and played a necessary role, satisfied the need for community.

By the time of the Industrial Revolution in the early 1800s, urbanization had taken hold. Many towns and villages became booming metropolises. For millions this brought a new-found interdependence. As time progressed, many people no longer grew their own food or made their own clothes or built their own houses. Few fixed their own plumbing or disposed of their own garbage. People became more and more dependent on others to survive.

Today, however, we no longer know very well the faces or names of the people we depend on to support our daily routine, and we are increasingly losing sight of what French sociologist Emile Durkheim called our "collective conscience." In our era, our division of labor has transformed the way we view our relationships with others.[2] We have come to deny our social connections and begun to see others as a specialized function rather than as neighbors. The bus driver is the bus driver, not Peggy. The doctor is the doctor, not Steve. And the farmer, well, we rarely see or hear about the person who grows what we eat—we just assume she's doing all right. We've got our food, but we tend not to wonder how it got to us. The mentality of new independence is based on a false perception. If anything, globalization has made us more connected to our neighbors around the world than ever before. We're often simply too focused on ourselves to see the ties.

In our interconnected world, our "social identity" is an even greater aspect of our personal identity. We identify ourselves with a wider social group, saying, "I am American" or "I am Canadian," or "I am black," or "I am Hindu," or "I am a tree hugger," or "I am a conservative." The answer to the question "Who am I?" is rooted in social identity as well as personal identity. In the broadest terms, people who feel a sense of community acceptance, social identity, and group purpose are more grounded and centered in their lives, and therefore happier. This is something very intrinsic to human nature. When people sense that they have a role to play in a wider community, they have a reason for being. In his classic study *Suicide*, Emile Durkheim found that people who face the breakdown of social norms and bonds, partially caused by a lack of *collective conscience* in our industrial society, are more likely to commit suicide than those with a stronger social network.[3]

Dr. Dorothea Gaither, a Toronto clinical psychologist, observed that she has never met a suicidal volunteer. "They don't kill themselves on Monday when they know they will be needed at their volunteer placement on Tuesday," she explained. Feeling needed by someone else often gives new meaning to the depressed person. They feel a sense of connection, an obligation, and a reason to continue living. Much of her work with the depressed, anxious, and physically ill is focused on helping them find meaning in their lives. This is often accomplished when people working with her begin to feel they are part of something larger than themselves and begin to focus on individuals around them who need help. Helping others, and the sense of community that comes with it, can literally be a lifesaver.

There is a body of literature that argues that our tendency to be individualistic, especially during times when our self-security is being threatened, is as natural as the imperative to be part of a community. We agree that there is a fundamental human instinct to self-preservation. This fact needs little listing of scientific proof. We have seen plenty of evidence in our culture of the desire to put the "self" first. The question we are posing isn't about self-preservation at its most basic level, but instead, about whether we need to help others to thrive and to develop to our fullest potential.[4]

We could continue to quote scientists, list studies, and present facts to prove that humans are by nature social beings (if your thirst for statistics and long words remains unquenched, just check out the endnotes). But does it really matter what these studies say? Ask yourself: Do you feel part of a larger group—a family, a faith group, a community, a nation? Do you feel a desire to see that group successful and happy? Do you feel that we are stronger together? Do you feel that we need each other to thrive?

BACK TO SESAME STREET

How do we start building communities? First, we recall a lesson from the voices of our childhood—Big Bird, Cookie Monster, and Grover, the friendly faces on Sesame Street—who remind us of the importance of knowing, appreciating, and interacting with the "people that we meet each day." If this were the norm, the late Mr. Hooper would have been proud. But we also need to be thinking of the people in our *global neighborhood*. We need to think and care about the people whom we don't meet, or haven't met until now, whom we once considered outside of our lives and experiences.

When Marc was 18 years old, he traveled overseas for the first time to volunteer in the slums of Thailand. He was to spend nearly eight months in one of Bangkok's largest slums, Klong Toey—a few acres of "unofficial land" where multitudes of people were forced to build their lives on what the city had forgotten. They lived in dim, creaking shacks pieced together from planks and rusted sheets of metal. They slept under the heavy blanket of fumes from the mounds of garbage around their homes. They brought their children up amidst poverty, disease, prostitution, and drugs, struggling to shield them from the worst of it.

When Marc first arrived in Klong Toey, he learned that one of his volunteer positions was to teach in a primary school. These children of the slum were to be his pupils. Overwhelmed by the mass of human desperation he saw around him, he wondered what lessons he could possibly offer that would help them to survive in this place, and why they would want to take notes from someone like him, who had never been forced to struggle in this way. Marc was stationed in what was known as the "Slaughter House" district of the slum. The name took on a clearer meaning on his first night there, when he awoke at 1:00 am to the sounds of animals being butchered in the next building. Every five minutes until dawn, their shrill screams tore through the stillness, and ripped at the courage and resolve that had brought Marc to this place.

The next morning, he reported shakily to the volunteer coordinator, a woman named Pi-Jai. She welcomed him with open arms and led him by the hand into the main street of the slum community. She stopped nearly everyone she passed, taking time to explain who Marc was and why he was there. By late afternoon, Marc began to worry that they were wasting time with the introductions. It felt wrong to be socializing when so much work needed to be done. But Pi-Jai told him that these introductions were important because they made Marc a member of the community, and only then could he volunteer within it. Once everyone knew him, they would protect him, and be willing to accept his help in return.

In the weeks that followed, Marc felt his initial uncertainty falling away. As he made his way to his volunteer placements throughout the slums, people would constantly wave at him, stop and shake his hand and in the little English they knew, ask him how we was, offer him food or water during lunch time, or walk him to his destination if he was lost. The kindness and generosity of the local people helped Marc to feel at home, and gave him a sense of real connection, purpose, and belonging in a community where he did not even speak a word of the language. Without this community-building experience, he might have viewed Klong Toey from the point of view of what it lacked: running water, electricity, proper sanitation. Certainly life in the slum was extremely difficult for its inhabitants, but Marc had discovered the incredible wealth of spirit within this community. These people felt a genuine and powerful connection to each other and to those who reached out to join them, and a deep appreciation for even the smallest things in life. Inspired by the feeling that he was part of something larger than himself, Marc decided to extend his volunteer work in the slum, staying months longer than he had originally planned.

Herein lies the key to creating community: helping others. By adopting the *Me to We* philosophy, we immediately enter an environment of mutual support and collaboration—we immediately build a community. To better understand how this works, we turn to New York University professor Thomas Bender's definition of a community, which includes "shared understandings and a sense of obligation. Individuals are bonded together by affective or emotional ties rather than by a perception of individual self-interest. There is a 'we'-ness in community."[5]

As we redefine what community means to us, we must reach outwards to an inclusive new dynamic that will allow us to attain our highest collective potential. In our own view, community includes everyone—family and friends, neighbors, members of our faith (and, for that matter, members of other faiths and of no faith), the convenience store clerk, and even the homeless person on the street or a continent away.

Many of us, however, have a peripheral sphere of compassion. We relate to and care for people depending on where they fall within our lives: our self; loved ones and family; the community immediately surrounding us; ethnic group or faith community; town or city; national; then international (to which we feel the least connected and the least responsible). Many of us find it easier to respond to the poverty of children in our own neighborhood than to hungry children suffering on another continent, but both are deserving of our compassion. Because we live in the era of globalization, and because we are human, we are connected not only to the people who immediately surround us, but also to people in other parts of the world. To build a strong and vibrant community, we have to make a conscious effort to widen our sphere of compassion and to recognize our responsibility to everyone who directly or indirectly is connected to us.

As author Dr. M. Scott Peck notes, "The enemy of community is exclusivity."[6] In the past, people created community around a particular geographic area, a religion, a nation, an ideology—but this has always created "in-groups" and "out-groups." The very fabric that bonded these people together to create community, by definition, also excluded others. We are seeking a fundamentally new definition of community—one that includes *everyone*, that rallies people of every culture, language, gender, religion, and way of life, to come together to help each other and to recognize that we are part of a whole.

In *Building Communities from the Inside Out*, John Kretzmann and John McKnight state that "communities cannot be rebuilt by focusing on their needs, problems, and deficiencies. Rather, community-building starts from the process of locating the assets, skills, and capacities of residents, citizens associations and local institutions."[7] This means that we must each look for gifts and talents that we can bring to the table to empower the entire group. This model allows us to celebrate and embrace differences among members of the community, because a diversity of skills, talents, knowledge, and experience is necessary to complete and sustain the whole.

The strength of the *Me to We* philosophy lies in the sense of connectedness it allows us to build with each other—whether with one person, a group of friends, or our broader surroundings. Through this connection, we become stronger as individuals and collectively as a community. A philosophy called Democratic Communitarianism recognizes that "individuals are realized only in and through communities, and that strong, healthy, morally vigorous communities are the prerequisite for strong, healthy, morally vigorous individuals."[8]

As we have seen, there is a natural tendency toward interaction and community in the animal kingdom; in the Masai, Puruhae, and other cultures around the world; and in the small yet powerful actions taken for others by individuals in our own society. We yearn for social contact with others from birth. Once we see that our lives have purpose and meaning beyond ourselves, we will have taken one large step forward to finding the elusive path to success and happiness.

COMMUNITY BUILDING *IS* POSSIBLE

Sometimes it requires a great tragedy to reveal our desire, need, and ability to create community. On September 10, 2001, Craig was attending a meeting across the street from the World Trade Center. That day, the financial district in New York City was engrossed in its business as usual—deal-making—whereby billions of dollars changed hands. The next morning, of course, the morning of 9/11, everything changed. Stranded in the city for over a week because of canceled flights, Craig came to see a very different New York City. Moved by the grief and shock of the attacks, New Yorkers came together in an unprecedented display of solidarity and mutual support. The attack was one of the most devastating acts of terror in modern history, but it also, conversely, served to bring out the best in people and to renew one's faith in humanity. Thousands of volunteers rushed to Ground Zero to bring blankets or coffee to the rescue workers, donate blood, or help with the search. In the days that followed, New Yorkers did not honk their horns while driving, doors were being held open for each other en masse, and strangers in the street stopped to talk to share the latest news. One of the many lasting images in Craig's memory of that week was that of a disheveled homeless person and a man in a stylish business suit, standing side by side, in a candlelight vigil in the area surrounding Ground Zero.

The entire country and much of the world came together in mutual grief and support. Millions of people were inspired by acts of generosity and kindness. For example, east coast communities in Canada played host for several days to large numbers of Americans who found themselves stranded on redirected planes. They opened up their hearts, kitchens, and spare bedrooms—and created lasting friendships. In Inez, Kentucky, a town where 40 percent of the children are from homes with incomes below the federal poverty level, elementary school students dropped coins into containers to help support the families of victims of the tragedy, giving anything they could afford. Meanwhile, thousands of Free the Children members across North America also got together to collect school and health supplies, winter coats, and blankets for the children of Afghanistan, who were forced to flee their homes and become refugees during the conflict in their country.

Now that time has passed since 9/11, it may seem that most Americans have largely returned to the temperament and priorities of September 10, 2001; however, many New Yorkers will tell you that they will never be the same. For a period of months, millions worked side by side to embody the pendulum shift from *Me to We*. If this type of mutual support is possible in New York City, then it is possible anywhere.

My Story

DR. JANE GOODALL

I started my life's work when I traveled to Africa, met Louis Leakey, and was given an amazing opportunity to learn about and learn from the chimpanzees. For decades now, I have studied these remarkable creatures. I always knew that animals had personalities, minds, and feelings. My work with the chimpanzees enabled me to convince scientists and many theologians that this was so.

Chimpanzees also demonstrate altruism. I remember on one occasion, Mel, a three-and-a-quarter-year-old infant chimpanzee, was adopted by a 12-year-old adolescent male, Spindle. When Mel's mother died, we thought Mel had no chance of surviving. With no siblings, he was completely alone in the world. We were amazed when Spindle adopted him. He allowed Mel to ride on his back or cling to his belly during travel, reached to gather the infant into his nest at night, shared his food, and did his best to keep Mel out of the way of adult males when they were socially aroused. Spindle saved Mel's life.

On a number of occasions, captive chimpanzees have risked their lives to save group members who fell into water-filled moats—for chimpanzees cannot swim. I especially remember one incident in which an adult male chimpanzee drowned as he tried to save an infant that was not his own.

There are a number of grave threats to the continued survival of chimpanzees. Deforestation, logging, hunting, and above all the bush meat trade threaten their survival in the natural world. My concern for these animals has led me into a major effort to educate people about our fundamental connection to and need for nature. Each aspect of the work in which

I am involved—education, poverty alleviation, community-based conservation, and conflict resolution—is interlinked, much like ecosystems themselves.

If we start to think about all that is wrong in the world, the picture is so grim that it may become difficult to take any action at all. "What can I, one individual out of more than six billion, do that will have any meaning?" We give in to the feeling of helplessness. Instead, we should concentrate on what we *can* do. The truth is that it is not possible to live through a day without having an impact on the world around us, either in a positive or a negative way. We all have a choice about the kind of difference we want to make. In our families, schools, communities, and cities, there are many problems that we can tackle, perhaps alone, perhaps with a friend or two. When we see that this effort does indeed make a difference, it gives us strength to do more.

This is the whole premise of Roots and Shoots, the environmental organization that I founded for young people. Everyone can make a difference in his or her own way. And when you learn that all around the world, thousands of other people also are working hard to make a difference, suddenly you are filled with hope. Every time I meet someone who is tackling a seemingly impossible task and refusing to give up, or living an inspirational life in the midst of poverty or other hardship, I learn something more about the power of the human spirit.

Chapter 7:

SEARCHING FOR MEANING, HAPPINESS, AND SUCCESS

"The purpose of life is a life of purpose."
— Robert Byrne —
(b. 1930)
Author

The *Me to We* philosophy creates a shift in how we think about life. For those who adopt it, it is an intensely personal experience that goes to the very soul of who we are. It leads us to think about what is truly important to us, to make new decisions about the way we want to live, the goals that we set for ourselves, the values that guide us, and the legacy that we want to leave for our children. Above all, it creates new ways of measuring meaning, happiness, and success in our lives, and makes these elusive goals finally attainable.

FINDING MEANING

When we traveled to Sierra Leone, West Africa, we discovered the most extraordinary human courage, resilience, and compassion. Of all the people whom we met during our visit, we will never forget the Mafinder family.

As the ten-year-long civil war ravaged Sierra Leone, this family fled their home and began the journey, on foot, to neighboring Guinea, where they hoped to find asylum. On the way, however, they came across a band of rebel soldiers who were traveling from village to village, destroying everything in their path. Upon seeing the convoy of soldiers approaching them, the family hid in the brush alongside the road–trying not to make a sound. But the youngest daughter, Hanna, who was six years old, was so afraid that she cried out. The rebels captured the three children–Hanna, John, who was nine years and old, and Suzanne, 11–and their grandmother. The parents managed to escape.

The rebels quickly decided that the grandmother was too old for manual labor, so she was shot to death. The children were then divided among them as trophies–the boy was given to one rebel commander and the two girls were given to another.

John was made to work as a slave in the fields for three years, helping to grow crops to feed the troops. As soon as he turned 12 years old, he was forced to become a soldier. He helped to transport diamonds from the diamond mines throughout Sierra Leone to secret rendezvous points, where, he explained, white men who spoke English would land their hel-icopters and trade guns for diamonds.

The two daughters were used as domestic servants by a rebel commander. After two years in captivity, they gave up hope of ever seeing their family again. But their father had never stopped looking for them. One day, at great personal risk, he crossed the border from Guinea into the rebel-controlled territory in Sierra Leone, searching for his missing children.

The father located the home where his daughters were being held captive. He met with the rebel commander and pleaded for their return. The commander, impressed with the father's determination and bravery, responded by saying that he could have one daughter back–and the other would be kept as a slave. The commander told the father to choose between Suzanne and Hanna.

The father broke down in tears, unable to choose which daughter would be free and which one would remain a slave. Suzanne was 13 years old at the time. She spoke on her father's behalf and told the commander that she would stay if he freed her younger sister, Hanna. Because of Suzanne's sacrifice, Hanna was granted her freedom and was permitted to leave with her father.

Every night Suzanne dreamed of escaping—but knew that if she were caught, the penalty would be death. Three months later, Suzanne was washing the clothes of the rebel commander at the riverbank when a woman approached her. This woman said that she was a friend of her family and that she would help Suzanne to escape.

That evening, Suzanne snuck out of the house and traveled with the woman under the cover of night. They slept during the day, hidden in the bush. When they approached the Guinea border, this woman gave Suzanne all the money in her possession—2,000 *leons*, the equivalent of one U.S. dollar—a fortune for people living in absolute poverty during the war. She told Suzanne to use the money to bribe the border guard. Then the woman disappeared.

When Suzanne approached the impasse between the two countries, she saw that the Sierra Leonean side of the border was controlled by rebel troops. One of the young boys—a child soldier—recognized her as a domestic servant and stopped her from crossing the border. The boy demanded to know why she was so far away from the commander's home. Suzanne, certain that the child soldier would kill her, showed him the 2,000 leons. She said that the money was given to her by the commander in order to buy shoes for him in Guinea and that she was to bring them back across the border to Sierra Leone. No slave would have had any money, so the boy believed her story and let her cross. Suzanne walked safely into Guinea—and to freedom.

Weeks later, Suzanne found the refugee camp and was reunited with her family. She never again saw the woman who had rescued her. In her five years of captivity, Suzanne had never encountered anyone who provided her with aid. Yet she was granted her freedom three months after trading her life to help her sister. To this day, she still believes that the woman was an angel–a miracle–sent by God, to help her.

We have visited some of the poorest and most challenging places in the world–Bosnia, Chiapas, the Middle East, Northern Ireland, Sierra Leone–and have witnessed terrible human suffering, the product of abject poverty and the societal impact of horrendous crimes against humanity, including genocide. We have met aid workers, some of whom have become so discouraged that they have simply given up on the world because of what they face every day. They find themselves questioning the very meaning of existence.

One of the greatest tragedies of the 20th century was the horror of the Holocaust. More than 11 million people perished during that period due to starvation, disease, and mass execution. Viktor Frankl was supposed to have been one of those numbers. He was put into a concentration camp and robbed of everything dear to him: his possessions, career, family, freedom, and the right to live or die. But his oppressors could not rob him of his soul. In his book, *Man's Search for Meaning*, he described Nazi camp guards, the torture and killings, but he also wrote of prisoners sharing their last piece of bread and walking through the bunkhouse to comfort their fellow captives.

The extraordinary examples of both cruelty and compassion led Frankl to conclude that in the final analysis, "everything can be taken from a man but ... the last of the human freedoms–to choose one's attitude in any given set of circumstances, to choose one's own way."[1] He believed that the greatest of these choices is the commitment to fulfill one's own sacred and unique task in life; by doing so, one could achieve one's highest potential: "Life ultimately means taking the responsibility to find the right answer to its problems and to fulfill the tasks which it constantly sets for each individual."[2] This is a path of love: "Love is the ultimate and the highest goal to which man can aspire... The salvation of man is through love and in love."[3]

Frankl's writings on the meaning of life have deeply influenced our personal beliefs. The *Me to We* philosophy is essentially a choice of how we live our lives. We have the freedom to choose how we respond to the worst of human situations, as we do to the minor problems of everyday life. Every time we witness pain, need, or injustice, we are challenged to be true to our values and to fulfill our most basic human instinct to help others. And at the core, what moves us to act is "love." While this may be an overused word, it is clearly an underused action. The *Me to We* philosophy seeks to correct this imbalance, to break down our barriers and bring us back to what is fundamentally human. To say that life's purpose is found in love may sound simplistic, but does it have to be more complicated?

Our personal beliefs on the meaning of life are best captured by a simple Jewish proverb:

> When we come into the world, we are crying and those around us are smiling. Our goal should be to lead our lives in such a way that when we leave, we are smiling and those around us are crying.

We should be content with the life that we have lived, and others should be sad to see us go because of the difference we have made in their lives.

ON BEING HAPPY

"The secret to happiness lies in knowing this: that we live by the law of expenditure. We find the greatest joy not in getting, but in expressing what we are ... The happy person is the one who lives by the life of love ..."
– Alfred North Whitehead –
(1861–1947)
Philosopher

Ten years ago, Chris Delaney was a star player on the football team at Bowling Green State University in Ohio. He had the talent and the drive to become a professional athlete. When he started missing catches, no one could blame it on lack of skill. Chris went to the doctor, thinking he needed glasses. Instead, he was diagnosed with a rare eye disease that could eventually leave him totally blind. He was devastated. Each morning, his vision seemed to get a little worse. Each night, he tried to escape through parties and drinking. He couldn't understand why this had happened to him.

One day he was pedaling his stationary bike, imagining his old days on his motorcycle, which he had loved so much. He missed the rush of the wind on his face. He'd never have that feeling again. He thought about all the long waiting lists for services for the blind, and wondered why no one raised money for the cause the way they did for cancer and AIDS. And then he surprised himself by asking: "Why not me?" The more he considered it, the more he knew it was what he had to do.

Chris set out to bike across the country–from the Pacific to the Atlantic Ocean–to heighten awareness about eye disease and raise funds for eye research. It would be an extremely difficult marathon because of his vision impairment, but he was determined. When he struggled through the pouring rain or labored over the steep terrain of the Rockies, it was the thought of helping others that encouraged him. People drove with their children alongside him to thank him and show him their support. As long as Chris could inspire others, he knew he would keep striving to do his best. After three long months, when he finally dipped his front wheel into the Atlantic Ocean, he discovered that he had raised $250,000 for the cause. Chris was filled with a sense of pride and accomplishment he had never felt before, not even on the football field. He went on to launch a speaking tour and to establish athletic programs for disabled children.

Today, Chris works with us full time, and he is one of our most valuable staff members. He is a great organizer—confident and compassionate, with a wonderful sense of humor. He believes that what happened to his eyes is God's way of telling him that this is what he must do with his life. In working to help others, Chris was able to make peace with himself and the ordeal he was forced to go through, and to find a way of life that gives him a sense of purpose and joy.

In their efforts to define happiness, some of the world's greatest leaders and thinkers have come to the simplest conclusion. Happiness is finding meaning in our lives through our contributions and service to others. As Dr. Albert Schweitzer, one of the greatest humanitarians of our time, once remarked: "One thing I know; the only ones among you who will be truly happy are those who have sought and found how to serve."

Psychologist David Myers, who has done extensive research on the source of happiness, asserts that happiness is rooted in key attitudes and practices. Although it may in part be determined by genes, it is something that we can generally control by taking care of our bodies and souls and nurturing close relationships. He encourages us to open ourselves, not only to people in our lives, but also to our own spiritual beliefs and understanding of God. He suggests keeping a *gratitude journal* and encouraging our children to do the same, to reflect each day on the things that we are thankful for in life: friends, family, freedom, and health and the brighter moments that made our day special. It is easy to become complacent about our blessings. Reaching out to others and sharing who we are in a meaningful way provides a source of support and joy, and a sense of self-worth.[4]

Our own definition of happiness evolved over time. We found (and continue to find) happiness in a nice meal, a good movie, a vacation, watching the occasional hockey game, and other such simple pleasures. But we discovered that a lasting sense of happiness had to be sought on a deeper level.

Initially, whenever we traveled, we brought back a piece of artwork to help remind us of our trip. After years of frequent travel, we had assembled quite a collection of knick-knacks. Most of them were not elaborate—small items that we would place on our desk—but soon they started overflowing our spaces. When we began to lose track of which carving came from which country, we realized that these trinkets were not helping to bring back the best memories of our travels—the happiest of which we had found in the people we met, the friendships we formed, the good laughs, stories, and adventures enjoyed together.

Since then, we have started investing in a different kind of memory; one that truly captures what our visit meant to us. Instead of a painting or small carving, we put aside some of our personal money to help someone in the country—money for medicine for someone who is sick, or for buying a school uniform for a child, or for giving a cow to a family as a permanent source of income. Whenever we look at the pictures of people we helped we remember our meeting, the happiness of the moment comes flooding back—the hugs, tears, and the joy we shared. Even years later, we can't help but smile.

In searching for your own definition of happiness, you may want to seek inspiration from the residents of the Klong Toey slum in Bangkok, Thailand, who measure happiness in small, simple ways. We recently visited Klong Toey to bring a group of North American students to volunteer at a center for street children. Many of the children had been taken in by the center at a very young age, having been orphaned or abandoned by parents who couldn't afford to care for them. One day, we saw the staff icing an enormous birthday cake. When we asked whose birthday it was, we were told that the celebration was for *all* the children. None of the street kids knew when they were born; some didn't even know their age. So once a year the center held a birthday party for all the children together. There was dancing and singing—laughing and story telling—a real celebration. The gathering created a sense of belonging for these children who have never known true family. The mountain of presents that we usually find at North American parties was absent, but the joy we saw in the room that day would be difficult to match. We played games with the children and sang songs in both English and Thai. We feasted on wonderful specialties donated by local people, and all the children happily lined up for a spoonful of birthday cake from their House Mother. One of the most precious moments for us was seeing one of our volunteers holding a young street child who was born HIV positive, and helping him to dance on "his birthday." The smile on the little boy's face is something we will never forget.

Sometimes true happiness waits for us in the most unlikely places; we only have to be willing to look for it—to be open and to share. There are no limitations—even a child living and dying with AIDS in one of the poorest slums in the world can find a reason to celebrate with others. If he can find happiness, anyone can.

ON THE PATH TO SUCCESS

"If I have been of service, ... if I am inspired
to reach wider horizons of thought and action,
if I am at peace with myself,
it has been a successful day."
— Alex Noble —

One person to whom we always look for advice as we go through life is our grandmother. At 90 years of age, she is truly a remarkable woman, with a small frame and a big loving smile. For 20 years she worked in the office of a major car manufacturer, where she became the head of her department. She did not have an easy life and had to work very hard to provide for our mother and her three siblings, as our grandfather died at an early age.

Ever since we were small children, we remember how our grandmother always had so many people around her. To this day, she is loved by everyone who knows her. She is a vibrant woman with a sparkle in her eyes; she still reads the newspaper every morning to keep up with current events. She lives alone in her home of many years, taking care of not only herself, but also everyone else in the neighborhood. They, in turn, all keep a watchful eye on her. When someone is sick, she is the first to visit with a friendly word or a pot of soup. When the workers from the post office next door to her home were on strike during the winter not too long ago, she brought them warm pots of coffee, freshly baked cookies, and words of support as they walked the picket line.

There is nothing our grandmother likes better than walking her dog every day and stopping to look at the trees and flowers that line her street, chatting with the neighbors she happens upon, or feeling the warm sun on her face. At her age, she knows that these are the many small pleasures that may soon be taken away from her.

We recently interviewed her for this book in search of her reflections on happiness and the meaning of life. "I think that we are all born for a purpose," she said. "We have a job to do in our own place and time in history. I often find myself thinking back and asking if I fulfilled that purpose. But it is a little late for me at 90 years of age. You have to ask yourself those questions when you are younger." She went on to tell us that the one lesson she learned in her many years is "being rich is a state of mind." She has seen countless people go through life "obsessed about collecting things that eventually sit in a closet or collect dust in a garage." She explained that if she had done this, no one would care about her today. She would be alone, with only a house full of trinkets to keep her company. She told us, "Measure your success by the number of hugs you give and smiles you bring to people's faces." Our grandmother never had a lot of money, but she is the richest person we know.

What exactly do we seek when we chase after "success"? When we host leadership workshops with adults or youth audiences, we ask them to list the most successful people of our time. In hundreds of sessions, the names most frequently on the list are those of people such as Nelson Mandela, Martin Luther King, Mahatma Gandhi, Terry Fox, and Rosa Parks.

According to the norms of our current self-help culture, these heroes would be considered failures. They did not reach their goals: racism still exists in the world, and inequality is still rampant. But these leaders lived by a community-based *We* philosophy, knowing that they were not acting alone and that their struggle would be carried forward by others. In the same way, the *Me to We* philosophy does not seek to measure individual success, but rather collective success—how "we" work together to reach our shared potential or to advance toward a common goal.

We believe that the mark of success is leaving a lasting legacy. This does not mean having a street named after you, building a statue with your face on it, or founding a company with your initials. Few can remember the names of the kings and queens of history. Statues crumble. Even the pyramids are covered by the sands of time. A true legacy is a living legacy. Every time a person of color sits at the front of a bus, we see the legacy of Rosa Parks. Every time a woman is appointed to the Canadian Senate, we see the legacy of The Famous Five.[5] If you have been important in the life of a child, you have left a legacy. If you have brought purpose, meaning, and joy to your family, you have left a legacy. Think about it: Mother Teresa's *mother* lived an amazingly successful life. Nelson Mandela's *father* did as well.

We cannot all be a Nelson Mandela or a Mother Teresa. The world could not function unless each one of us had different talents and skills. We need scientists, teachers, artists, garbage collectors, carpenters, and economists, as everyone makes an important contribution to the working of a healthy society. The secret of success is having lived a life larger than ourselves. People will be ultimately remembered by how they chose to use their gifts and talents and how they touched the lives of others.

One person who strove to leave a legacy was Alfred Nobel, the founder of the Nobel Prize. Nobel made his fortune as the inventor of dynamite. One day, his brother died and the local newspaper got the brothers mixed up and mistakenly reported that Alfred, himself, was the one who had passed away. Reading his own obituary in the paper the next day, Alfred was shocked by what he saw. Much of the article dealt with the destruction and death caused by his invention. That very moment, he was moved to rewrite his own obituary and to leave a positive legacy in the world. He decided to leave his fortune to the establishment of the Nobel Prizes, including the famed Nobel Peace Prize, to celebrate the creative forces of all humanity.

You don't have to win a Nobel Prize to leave a legacy. Just make the world a better place today, for even one person. For our grandmother, that legacy is the care, the encouragement, and the joy she brought to her family, and the importance she played in all of our lives. This type of success can never be taken from you and lives on as a testament to your contribution. Perhaps Ralph Waldo Emerson said it best:

To laugh much; to win respect of intelligent persons and the affections of children; to earn the approbation of honest critics and endure the betrayal of false friends; to appreciate beauty; to find the best in others; to give one's self; to leave the world a little better, whether by a healthy child, a garden patch, or a redeemed social condition; to have played and laughed with enthusiasm, and sung with exultation; to know even one life has breathed easier because you have lived, this is to have succeeded.

My Story

OPRAH WINFREY

I will never forget the year I was about 12 years old, living with my mother who was single and raising my half-sister, my half-brother, and me in Milwaukee. We were on welfare, and she told us that we would not be receiving Christmas gifts because there was not enough money. I remember at the time that I felt sad and thought: What will my story be? What would I say when the other kids asked what I'd gotten? What will my classmates think when I go back to school and say, 'We didn't have Christmas because we didn't have any money.' Just when I started to accept that there would not be a Christmas that year, three nuns showed up at our house with gifts for all of us. There was a turkey, a fruit basket, and some games, and for me, they brought a doll. I felt such a sense of relief that I had been given something, and that I would no longer have to be embarrassed when I returned to school. I remember feeling that I mattered enough to these nuns—who I had never met and to this day still do not know their names—and what it meant that they had remembered me. I wasn't forgotten. Somebody had thought enough of me to bring me a gift.

Years later, in the spring of 2002, I stood in the kitchen of my new house and thought about that upcoming Christmas, envisioning how I wanted to decorate the house to make my first Christmas there special and memorable. I then started to think about the best Christmas I ever had, and I instantly recalled the nuns' visit and impact they had on my life. I have always encouraged giving, using your life, teaching what you learn, and extending yourself in the form of service. So, that day in my kitchen, I put that same challenge to myself. What could I do, by using the abundance that I had been blessed with, to make this Christmas more meaningful to someone else? I decided that I wanted to create that same feeling of importance and acknowledgement for as many children as I could possibly reach. I immediately thought of the children of South Africa, whose poverty and suffering I had seen firsthand on my previous visits. The people of South Africa and the strength of their spirit had always held a special place in my heart. I simply wanted to create one day in the lives of these children that they could remember as a happy one.

So, I came up with a plan and gathered 40 people from my company, Harpo, Inc., to help. Together with my greatest living mentor, Nelson Mandela, we created a program that I called Christmas Kindness South Africa 2002. We worked together to identify gifts that would be culturally relevant from black dolls—which none of these children had ever seen—and soccer balls, which is one of South Africa's favorite sports, to sneakers for every child, because so many of them don't own a pair of shoes. We wanted to help these children forget their troubles and have some fun, even if only for a short while. We created a fantasyland of parties—complete with Christmas trees, fairy princesses and jesters, games, and prizes—for the orphans, most of whom had never attended a party in their lives. It was at the first one of these parties that I experienced the single greatest moment of my life.

We gathered approximately 125 children from different orphanages at each party. For every child, we wrapped colorful packages filled with toys, clothes, much-needed books, and school supplies. Each of their packages was labeled with their name. We wanted all of them to know they were special, and for a lot of those children it would be the only gift they had ever received. Before I called out their names and handed them their gifts, I reminded them that they couldn't unwrap their presents until every child had come forward. Much to my surprise, they sat patiently–like no other children I had seen before–for what must have seemed like an eternity, listening for their cue. Finally, the moment they had been waiting for came as I called out, 'One, two, three. Open your presents!' As the children ripped open their packages, their faces beamed as their jubilant smiles lit up the room. They cheered, sang, and danced in celebration. They hugged their gifts and hugged one another; the joy in the room was palpable, and it wasn't just about toys. It was a feeling–the feeling I knew from that Christmas so long ago when the nuns came to visit... I wasn't forgotten. Somebody thought of me. I matter.

I never knew that level of joy existed until that Christmas I spent with the children of South Africa. Their energy and elation was contagious. I felt it so deeply; it was overwhelming and it completely filled me. I realized in that moment that joy has a texture you can really feel. I saw myself in their eyes, and I carry their joy in my heart. I am grateful to God that I was able to see, touch, hear, and feel that kind of happiness by giving back to those who had so little. That Christmas we were able to bring joy to 50,000 children, but there were more than a million moments of happiness.

Making other people happy is what brings me happiness. This principle of living has brought me enormous good fortune, long before I knew this is how the Universe works. I grew up being taught: 'Do unto others as you would have them do unto you.' The real lesson is what you do to others will indeed be DONE unto you. What you put out comes back; it's the third law of motion. So we're always rewarded in kind according to the depth of our deeds. I speak daily to 10 million people all over the world with the purest intention of in some way lifting them up through hope, laughter, inspiration and entertainment. I, in turn, have been exalted by the blessings.

Chapter 8:

WITHIN "WE" IS "ME"

"So divinely is the world organized that every one of us,
in our place and time,
is in balance with everything else."
— Johann Wolfgang von Goethe —
(1749–1832)
Playwright

There is an old adage, "In order to help others, you must first help yourself." We respectfully disagree. It is not a question of first or second. We have met people in desperate personal need, but who, in reaching out to help others, gained for themselves the motivation and ability to improve their own situation. As these individuals bettered their personal lives, they sought to share their improved situation with friends, family, and community members. And in reaching out, they gained a renewed sense of purpose, energy, and optimism. It's a positive cycle of personal and collective uplifting. We believe the saying should be "In order to help others, you must *also* help yourself."

BEING WILLING TO TRUST AGAIN
Moving from *Me to We* is not easy for people who have opened themselves up in the past, only to have experienced pain and rejection. They may be afraid to let down their guard and try to rebuild the links of friendship and community. It can feel

safer to simply close oneself off to others to avoid being hurt once again. Some people find their souls in agony from the pain that life has inflicted—pain that has left them broken people—angry, filled with hate and with a desire for revenge. For millions, forgiveness is hard; to forget is impossible; and to risk again can be frightening.

We learned this during one of our trips to Sierra Leone. While walking to the market in Freetown, the capital city, with a boy who was an amputee, Marc was surprised to hear him say, "Over there, he is the one who chopped off my arm with a machete." In total disbelief, Marc watched the young man, no older than the victim himself, walking about freely in the market. How could this be? How could victims of such abuse be forced to face the perpetrators in their villages *every day*? How could they bear the pain?

It was Christine, a woman who oversees our schools in Sierra Leone, who introduced us to the notion of forgiveness and reconciliation—the only possible route for many people in their search for healing and peace. She shared with us the pain suffered by members of her own family—the rape of a 14-year-old niece, the abduction of a nephew forced to become a member of the rebel army, and the abuse suffered by a brother who had been taken prisoner for two years.

Christine is one of the most generous and alive people we have ever met. She gives of herself endlessly to help children, the old, and the suffering in Sierra Leone.

"How do you do it?" we asked. "How do you continue to serve and to help the very people who caused so much pain to you and to your family?"

Christine admitted that it was not easy. So many people in Sierra Leone had endured absolute hell—even more so because the hurt was often inflicted by family, neighbors, and people who lived in the same community. Many of the children who were abducted were forced to become soldiers and made to follow orders under threat of death, or drugged to make them more compliant to obey orders to mutilate and to kill.

Although Christine believes that truth and justice are important, she also understands that there is no future for Sierra Leone without forgiveness and compassion. After time, she said, you come to understand that hatred and bitterness can eat you alive. Living in anger and constantly seeking revenge is a punishment inflicted only on ourselves; it keeps us from healing past wounds and prevents us from moving forward. Christine has learned that trusting again may be more difficult than enduring the initial pain. But in moving forward and taking the risk to open herself up to others, she is able to live again and experience the joy that life can offer.

How many of us lead miserable lives because we feel we have been deeply hurt or wronged by a loved one, a co-worker, a neighbor, or a stranger? How often do we waste our chance for happiness by spending our lives clinging to pain, anger, and bitterness? Because of the faults of one or more people, we punish ourselves by not allowing ourselves to move forward, to trust again, to create new friendships and develop community bonds. As Jacques Lusseyran, blind from the age of eight and a World War II prisoner stated, "... Unhappiness, I saw then, comes to each of us because we think ourselves at the center of the world, because we have the miserable conviction that we alone suffer to the point of unbearable intensity. Unhappiness is always to feel oneself imprisoned in one's own skin, in one's own brain."[1]

Dr. Dorothea Gaither, a psychologist who works with people in pain, explained to us that forgiving and letting go first begin with an intellectual choice we make—by saying it out loud or writing it down. Then, it is a gradual process we work on over time. Hatred and negative emotions not only affect our health but also prevent us from living any kind of happy or meaningful life. We become victimized over and over again, every day. It is not a question of forgetting the pain or pretending it never happened but rather letting go of the hold that the other person or situation has on us. Forgiving releases that hold and allows our hearts to be free.

Reaching out from "me" and joining a larger community is not an easy step. It requires lowering our guard, approaching others with compassion, being willing to accept help—all of which are difficult. Sometimes, through service to others, we can find a way to give our suffering meaning in helping other victims of similar tragedies. Often, the issues that we think are major problems in our own lives are put into perspective as we see the courage of people who are in worse situations than ourselves. As we break down barriers, we open our lives to new and rewarding opportunities.

"YOU" IS CHARITY, "WE" IS PARTNERSHIP

It sometimes happens that although you are ready to make the step from *Me to We*, others around you may not be at the same stage. Perhaps these individuals were hurt in the past. Perhaps they are still having difficulty trusting, forgiving, and opening up. To make the move from *Me to We*, we have to prepare not only ourselves but those around us as well.

The movement from *Me to We* involves a risk: that someone you reach out to may not reach back. For example, you may try to help someone in need who actually denies that there's a problem, who tells you flat out, "No, thank you, I can manage just fine on my own." Or you may volunteer to help a group or an organization and find that your overture is turned down. The reality is that it's hard to know how people will react when you offer to help them. Many will appreciate your concern, but others may find it difficult to accept your help.

Pride can sometimes become an issue when your offer is interpreted as pity. No one wants to lose face.

For this reason, it's often more effective to approach people with the attitude of *partnership* rather than charity—the understanding that you both have an equal stake in their well-being. It is not "You need help." Instead, it is "We can solve this mutual problem together." When you respect the feelings as well as the input of the people you are trying to help, the result can be an empowering experience for everyone involved.

This approach has been enormously successful in our development work overseas and has helped us to form strong and lasting relationships with our project partners. For example, in the rural regions of Ecuador, this understanding broke down barriers with the Puruhae Indigenous communities with whom we wanted to build a number of primary schools.

For years, the Puruhae had been seen by many people as lesser citizens, unable to manage themselves and in need of handouts and charity. The truth is that they are a proud people who have had a difficult history and are currently facing even more trying circumstances. One can easily pity them or look down on them—their communities often lack clean water, schools, or even the most basic medical facilities. But realistically, it was only a generation ago that they escaped from a near slave-like system under the *hacienda* owners. In just one generation, they have completely transformed their lives and have managed to scrape out an existence on a barren landscape. They have an extraordinary work ethic; many of their members perform backbreaking manual labor, toiling 12 to 16 hours a day in the fields during harvest time. From the outset of our dealings with these people, we showed them that we valued their input and their knowledge, respected their traditions, and needed their active involvement to make the schools a reality.

International aid agencies often work with people in need by using one of two very different philosophies developed in their programs: "need-based" or "asset-based" approaches. "Need-based" development is how many charities help: by looking at people who are poor, neglected, or vulnerable and treating them like beggars, giving them something to eat or a handout of money. The "asset-based" approach is that of seeing the strengths of people. One builds on these strengths working with them. The Puruhae people are hard workers. Instead of asking for food, they asked for seeds and farming equipment. They would provide the labor. This approach is not just a hand-out; both groups work in partnership. Together, "we"–the Puruhae and us–are able to improve their situation.

Had we come with offers of charity, however, the Puruhae, having been neglected, subjugated, and oppressed for so long, would have naturally been cynical and suspicious of us. Had we treated them as weak or vulnerable, they would rightly have resisted our help. As a result, there would have been no schools in their communities, and we would have missed out on the valuable friendships and lessons that we gained while working alongside them.

On a personal level, this respect for others and sense of partnership is the difference between telling someone you want to help them because they have a lot of problems, or offering your support because you believe in their potential. It's the difference between telling a fellow that you will spend time with him because he seems lonely and asking him to go with you to a movie that you are both excited to see.

Not every individual or group that you approach will necessarily be willing or ready to engage in a partnership. Should you be turned down, it's important not to lose heart or forget what led you to reach out in the first place: a genuine concern for others and a desire to make a difference. This spirit of *Me to We* will keep your heart open and it will eventually connect you with people who will appreciate and value what you can bring to their lives.

FINDING A BALANCE

Over the years, we have seen organizations working on social issues come and go. Their leadership and members frequently get so caught up in their cause that they neglect other responsibilities in their lives. They spend late nights working, ignore their health, don't take personal time to recharge their batteries, and even put themselves in dangerous situations in their work overseas. Inevitably, the result is burnout, both physical and emotional.

When approached for advice by young people who are becoming involved in their community, we always tell them to find a balance. Neglecting their personal responsibilities at home, work, or school, or their own needs is a disservice both to themselves and to others. Helping others is not a sprint; it is a lifelong marathon. Both of us are often reminded of this by mentors we admire who are 70, 75, even 80 years old. They tell us to pace ourselves—this has been key to their lifetime of service.

The *Me to We* philosophy is not one of complete selflessness. It is meant to take care of the *Me* as part of the *We*—to uplift the individual as well as the group, to achieve a balance between our focus on the self and our actions to help others. We are not made like the Energizer™ bunny that "keeps going and going." We need to take time to re-energize our body spirit. When we allow ourselves to become physically, emotionally, and spiritually exhausted, everybody loses—including ourselves. Even Mother Teresa, who opened her heart and shouldered many people's problems, spent three hours every day in prayer, reflection, and meditation and insisted that all her nuns do the same. She believed that it was essential for them to take care of their body and their spirit if they were to live a life of intensive service to others without burning out.

For every person, the appropriate balance is different. Some find much-needed relaxation or change of pace in spending one evening a week at a Boy's or Girl's Club. Others may rejunenate their spirit by taking time at the end of the workday to make a nice meal with their spouse, by attending a play or a musical presentation, going to the gym, reading a book or taking their children to the park. In our work with young people at *Free the Children*, we always make it a point to get together after a meeting or leadership session to have some down time and fun. We also encourage our staff, who put in long hours every day, to take time off when they find themselves stressed, to go home and rest, to read and reflect, or to make a change in their routine.

It's okay to think about your own needs when reaching out to others. For example, picking your dream volunteer placement is not a selfish thing—when you do something that you love, you do it better and are able to help more people. When volunteering, think about which talents you want to develop. Find something uplifting and emotionally rewarding. Assess how much time you can commit without overburdening yourself. Above all, no matter what you do to reach beyond yourself, do it because you *want* to. Offering your assistance because you feel guilty or obligated will make you see helping others as a chore. And we did *not* write this book for *that* to happen.

This same balance exists in giving and receiving. On some days you might be able to offer a smile and a shoulder to a friend to lean on; on others days, you might allow a friend to return the favor and help you through a difficult time. There is no shame in accepting aid from another. To reject an overture is to take away from someone the opportunity to give. In accepting help, you provide the other individual with a gift in return. The cycle works only when we both open up ourselves to sharing *and* receiving.

The two of us have learned over the years how important it is to be open to other people sharing with us—both for our benefit and theirs. One of Craig's most cherished memories is of his visit to a very poor rural village near Xiuyan county in northeastern China for the opening ceremonies of two schools built by Free the Children. In one village, each family contributed one duck egg to a large box of eggs presented to Craig as a token of gratitude for their new school. In another village, the children gathered a wild edible green plant, a rare delicacy in many Chinese homes that grows high up on the side of mountains. In both cases, the students and their parents were just beaming with pride in giving their precious gifts to Craig because in these areas where poor soil and rocky terrain yield little in sustenance, food is scarce and very much treasured. It was important for these families to give something valuable to Craig, because they considered their schools such an important gift for the future of their children. In accepting these presents, Craig acknowledged their generosity and recognized them as equal partners in giving and receiving.

The beauty of the *Me to We* philosophy is that we create a world in which this balance is possible. It involves both giving and receiving. We improve the community and ourselves, and create a support network on which we can rely. We can best help others when we are in a positive frame of mind and healthy. In fact, the very essence of "we" prescribes this balance—the word "we" incorporates others and ourselves, both you and me.

My Story

KATHY BUCKLEY

I began my life—my real life—the day I died.

Of course, I didn't know it at the time, but that's how it went. I finally saw the light when I was run over by a Jeep.

Before that, my life was about as peachy as you'd expect when you look like a telephone pole, can't hear, and think you're mentally retarded. Add to that sexual molestation, a few more near-death experiences, and a bout with cervical cancer, and you get the picture. Not the best life on the planet.

So why am I laughing now? I'll tell you.

For as long as I can remember, life seemed, well, *confusing*. Everyone else seemed to have it so together. Not me. I didn't have a clue. It would have helped if someone had told me I was deaf. No one knew. Instead, they thought I was a smart-aleck kid with a weird voice, an unfortunate perm (what was my mom thinking?), and an annoying way of staring at people's lips.

I didn't know that others could hear more than the low rumblings and "wah-wah" sounds that I heard. Grown-ups told me I spoke funny because I had a lazy tongue. I'd stand in front of the mirror and poke my tongue, trying to wake it up. Somehow, I managed to teach myself to lip-read.

At school, I was completely lost. How do you read the teacher's lips when she's writing on the chalkboard? In second grade, the teacher started teaching phonics. "Sound it out, Kathy!" Uh … I don't think so.

Finally, someone thought to test my hearing. I'd been at that school for three years before anyone clued in to the fact that I was deaf. (And *they* called *me* slow!)

Just one little problem. They forgot to tell *me*.

Instead, they gave me these big plastic earmuffs: Zenith Diplomat hearing aids. I hated them. They must have had a pound of plastic for each ear. It was the only time in my life I was actually top-heavy. I didn't understand why I had to wear these stupid things. They sent me to a school for the disabled. I figured it was because I was causing trouble and they didn't want me there anymore.

It wasn't so bad at the new school. I made friends with a sweet little blind girl. I used to trade sandwiches with her. At least, I thought she knew we were trading. Later, I learned she never saw me make the exchange—just thought she was getting boring PB-and-J, while I got yummy barbecued beef. Of course, I never heard her complain!

At the special school I learned how to speak well enough to be sent back to the public system. With my big hearing aids, funny speech, and a growth spurt that shot me up to six feet tall, I felt like an alien. I wore a thick headband to hide the hearing aids and stole candy from my parents to make the other kids like me. All I was doing was looking for acceptance, a place to belong.

By high school I'd learned how to deflect attention with wisecracks. I didn't think I was being funny. Joking was my defense mechanism to keep them from seeing my pain, from seeing that I was dumb. If they laughed *with* me, they couldn't laugh *at* me. I became my own one-woman improv group.

Academically, I was a disaster. I don't know what I was thinking when I signed up for French. Try lip-reading "oui, oui." I didn't make it in typing either. I'd sit at the keyboard with my fingers in the air, ready to go, while everyone else was typing away. Apparently there was a record player going, dictating what we were supposed to type. Music class? Get that girl outta here! I graduated with a one-point grade average.

It wasn't much better after graduation. I couldn't hold a job because I kept messing up. As an employee in the fashion industry, I was asked to cut 15 patterns. I thought they said 1,500 and I was cutting for days. Job after job, I was fired, and I had no idea why.

I had a series of accidents—which I suspect were half-hearted attempts at suicide—and my mother kicked me out of the house at 18. I just kept thinking there was something wrong with me. Why couldn't I connect? "Fix me!" I wanted to cry. "Or just let me die." I kept imagining cutting my arm off and watching myself bleed to death. With a little blade I started scratching things into my arm. I just wanted the pain to stop.

One morning I decided to lie on the beach by myself. Suddenly, I saw a lifeguard's Jeep barreling across the sand. I thought to myself, "My God, the way that Jeep is tearing around someone is liable to get run over."

I never thought it would be me.

Run over by a lifeguard! Talk about not knowing your job description.

I felt terrible pressure as my body was pressed into the sand. This was very bad. But strangely, I felt okay—like I could finally be at peace—for just a moment. Then, *no!* I wasn't ready for this. Suddenly there was noise and paramedics and someone shouting "3:40, dead on arrival." A sheet was pulled over me. I couldn't move. I was strapped to a board, wearing a neck brace. I blew hard on the sheet to get it off my face. "I'm so sorry," someone kept saying.

I was in ICU for six days. It wasn't until later I realized what a gift I'd been given when I died—the gift of choice. I would use that gift much later to turn my whole life around. For the moment, all I knew was that I was alive—but might never walk again. I sat in the wheelchair looking out the hospital window and pleaded with God: "Please don't forsake me. I don't want to end up in a wheelchair for the rest of my life lip-reading nose hair."

One day, when I could finally use my legs again, I had a complete physical examination. Lo and behold, they diagnosed a hearing impairment! No, Kathy, the examiner said, you're not retarded. I tried my first pair of *functional* hearing aids. Keys jingled! The door squeaked! God knows how long that toilet's been running! I even heard myself pee. Scared me to death! I thought my liver had fallen out.

With the knowledge of my disability, I could feel those old labels start to fade. I found a job as a massage therapist. One morning a woman came in. She'd just been in a bad accident. Her body hurt; it was too tense to massage. Instead, I joked with her. "I was so mad at that guy for driving right out in front of me," she said. "Oh, be honest. You're pissed 'cause you missed your hair appointment." As she laughed, I could feel the pain and tension in her body fade away. That day, I saw the power of laughter. Until then, I'd just used it to keep people away.

Not long after, a friend dared me to take part in a stand-up comedy contest to raise money for children with cerebral palsy. What did I know about comedy? But then I remembered that day under the Jeep, and how I was given the gift of choice. Here was a choice I could make to help children. I'd do it. To my surprise, all the years of wisecracking paid off. I ended up in the semi-finals—me with my two weeks in the business up against 80 others who'd been comedians for three to ten years—and I placed fourth.

So you see, it was completely unplanned. I made a choice to reach out of my wallowing little world and ended up with a career making people laugh. I'm having a life I never thought I could have. I've written a book and an award-winning autobiographical play, and now have a successful career as a motivational speaker, sharing my stories of exclusion to help others.

Funny thing—every time I went onstage, I could feel something changing inside me. The monster that I used to feel crawling around in my stomach was withering away. With each speech, with each positive thought, or every time I reached out to another person, the monster got smaller.

I learned that wallowing is bad—but easy to do. And I learned that reaching out is good—and surprisingly easy too. It's as simple as stepping outside of "What about me" to "What about you...What do you need today that I can offer you? A smile, a hug?" If you put a smile on someone's face, you're going to feel better yourself.

What it comes down to, on a selfish level, is this: making people laugh gives me an opportunity to put a smile on my God's face. Every time I get to touch somebody's heart or their spirit, that smile may be God saying, "You did good today, honey."

Chapter 9:

HELPING OTHERS IS
GOOD FOR YOU

*"It is one of the beautiful compensations of this life that no one
can sincerely try to help another without helping himself."*
— Ralph Waldo Emerson —
(1803–1882)
Poet and Essayist

With the *Me to We* philosophy, we have come to a new definition of meaning, success, and happiness, and discovered how to create the community in which all these elements can be found. We've learned what helping others can do for society as well as our spirits, but what about the traditional benefits that most people are looking for when they turn to self-help books?

The best thing about the *Me to We* philosophy is that it strikes a balance between improving the self and others, and providing deeper, soulful rewards and tangible gains. In helping others, we can help ourselves at many levels. We benefit in our personal relationships, our health, our business, and our self-esteem—all of which for many of us are the elements of a better quality of life. Therefore, you, personally, and the world benefit at the same time.

HELPING OTHERS:
GOOD FOR THE WORLD VIEW
What happens when someone who grows up amid the excesses of North America travels to build a school in rural Africa?

Or volunteers at Mother Teresa's orphanages in India? Or works with children in need in their neighborhood?

Their lives are forever changed.

When she left her home in Seattle, Washington, to spend the summer volunteering at a center for street children in Bangkok, Thailand, 17-year-old Sonya Hetrick was not prepared for what she would witness. "Among the orphaned boys and girls who survived abandonment and molestation and things no child should ever have to go through, I found an inner strength that I can only hope to develop within myself," she wrote in her reflections. Following a volunteer experience teaching in Kenya, Olivier Lemay, a parent from Montreal, Quebec, remarked, "I had reached a stage in my life when I was searching for something more. I found it in the eyes of those kids."

The self-perception of young people who travel overseas to volunteer is enriched with a greater sense of purpose and heightened self-respect. This inner transformation is reflected in the increased confidence they have in their daily interactions with others and in the realization that they are part of something greater than themselves. Or it can be seen in something as simple as the participants having a reason to get up in the morning, eager to embrace the day and all that it offers. Whatever the motivation, they come to understand the power of their own contribution.

Allison Sander, a student at Lewis and Clark College in Portland, Oregon, returned from her trip to Africa "transformed." She left home as a shy teenager, confused about her life goals, and returned a confident young leader, firm in her mission to be part of the solution to the problems she had witnessed. Allison had learned that finding happiness in day-to-day life starts from within, from converting the quiet compassion she felt for others into real action. Like many young people who travel overseas to volunteer, when she returned she became more aware of problems in her own community and joined local organizations to help.

Many of our overseas volunteers are young people between the ages of 14 and 18. During the flight home there is, at times, a rush to the phone during the stopover in London to call their families and friends—not to catch up on gossip or express a craving for North American fast food, but to relate how the experience has changed them and how their lives and habits are going to be different. A few of the older participants have even called their boyfriends and girlfriends and broken up with them. Ending a relationship with Mr. or Ms. Wrong may seem like a small step; however, it's symbolic of a larger change. Many also call their parents to thank them for their support. In short, these young people do not want to go back to their old lives. Like Allison, these youths have a new vision of the world—and of themselves.

But you don't have to travel halfway around the world to find greater meaning or true happiness. These same positive experiences also take place when our local Free the Children chapters distribute sandwiches to homeless people on city streets in urban centers in North America. Volunteers inevitably reach the same conclusion: no matter what they are required to do—deliver food, dig a hole, teach a class, run around all day with children, organize a social justice campaign, or build a schoolroom—they receive far more than they give. They learn far more than they teach. They change their everyday attitudes, habits, and outlook on life far more than they ever dreamed they would. They have what Professor Phyllis Moen calls "enhanced psychological well-being" measured by "a sense of mastery over one's life, self-esteem, life satisfaction and energy level."[1]

HELPING OTHERS:
GOOD FOR RELATIONSHIPS

Bachelors and bachelorettes—good news! Volunteering can help you spot Mr. or Ms. Right pretty quickly as well. We joke in our office that we should close down and re-open as a dating agency. Many people who work with us have found their significant other while becoming socially involved—and that's after they have tried introduction services, Internet dating, and newspaper personals. Like magic, the love of their life appears while they're packing boxes of school kits or organizing a campaign to take action on a social issue. But there's nothing magic about it. Giving of your time and helping others is an enjoyable experience that puts you in touch with people who have common interests, passions, and values.

You don't have to find your soulmate, however, to enjoy the friendships you create through reaching out to others. We can just about guarantee that if you go to a retirement center and spend some time with a lonely woman, she will appreciate you more than anyone else in the world. If you decide to become a Big Brother or Big Sister to a troubled youth, he or she will value you not for how suave or rich or thin you are, but for the difference you are making in his or her life. In the self-help culture, many people hide their true selves or strive to be someone else in order to gain approval or be accepted by a particular circle of "friends." Genuine connections between people built on acceptance and compassion are often the antidote to the solitude and loneliness that so many people feel in their lives.

From our own experience, we have found that our family has become stronger through our work in helping others, despite the fact that we live in an age of weakening family structures. Both of our parents are retired teachers, and their regular volunteer work as adult mentors with Free the Children has allowed them to retain contact with young people, which has always been their true calling. This has also enabled us to spend more time together as a family, working side by side with a common purpose and vision that brings us closer together.

We have wonderful parents who have done everything they can to help us find our way in the world. But we have also been fortunate to meet some inspiring individuals who have taken us into their lives and provided us with the advice, encouragement, and support of true mentors. Helping others can frequently put you in touch with people who recognize your gifts and potential, and who can direct you to employment and leadership opportunities or provide you with a reference for a job or scholarship. We can't say enough about mentors. The many with whom we've been blessed over the years have exposed us to unique and wonderful experiences and helped to guide us on our life paths.

HELPING OTHERS: GOOD FOR BUSINESS
Through volunteer activities, people create bonds of friendship and trust, and these bonds often lead to formal relationships in the business and professional world. Potential employers see community service as an indication of team spirit and a positive attitude. Customers see companies reaching out to help the community as a sign of corporate social responsibility and good business ethics. The bottom line: helping is as good for the wallet as it is for the soul.

We have worked with Rotary Clubs around the world to bring charitable projects to developing countries, and we have a great deal of respect for this group. Rotary is one of the world's oldest secular service organizations established to bring together big-hearted people from various professions and cultures to build better local and global communities. Originally, one of the key principles of Rotary was that members would conduct business among themselves—they trusted each other and gave each other good deals, knowing that they wouldn't be cheated. The very name of Rotary was characterized by the fact that members would hold group meetings in different business locations, which would rotate every few weeks, thereby allowing all members to eventually display their products. Rotary even used to give out awards to those who bought and sold the most goods and services to fellow Rotarians. Today Rotary provides concrete proof that business success and charity are not mutually exclusive concepts.

The Young Presidents' Organization (YPO)[2] organized its 2004 Global Leadership Summit under the theme "Making a Difference." The chair of the organizing committee explained to us that the most successful members and companies in the network were the ones that promoted community service and provided philanthropy programs. It's not hard to understand why these same companies are constantly rated among the best companies to work for. When people feel valued and connected to a community, they find more meaning in their jobs, no matter what they do.

From Ben and Jerry's ice cream, to Paul Newman's salad dressings, to The Body Shop, more and more businesses are engaging in socially responsible ventures and becoming involved in the community. When Anita Roddick, activist, businesswoman, and founder of The Body Shop, took the company public in 1984, she pushed its mandate far beyond that of simply increasing profits, to raising social consciousness and global solidarity. Its mission statement opens with the overriding commitment to "dedicate our business to the pursuit of social and environmental change," proving to the corporate world that it is possible to combine profits with principles.[3]

Increasingly, consumers are voting with their dollars for ethical, responsible, and sustainable business practices. The *Globe and Mail's Report on Business* magazine released a survey called its "First Ever Corporate Social Responsibility Ranking" in March 2004, because it believed corporate social responsibility to be "the most important issue of the century ... so far."[4] In their assessment of the performance of Canada's top 1,000 profitable companies ranging in areas from environment to community relations to human rights, the authors cited a GlobeScan[5] public opinion poll that showed that 83 percent of Canadians believe that corporations have a social responsibility in addition to their traditional economic role. Moreover, 51 percent of those surveyed made the decision to not buy stocks or products from companies perceived to be socially irresponsible. Conversely, consumers are remaining loyal to companies that demonstrate good corporate citizenship in their communities, both locally and globally.

Not only can the CEO enjoy the benefits of the *Me to We* philosophy, even students looking for their dream job can reap the rewards. Volunteer experience can be added to their resumé for future job searches and improve their chances of getting into the college or university of their choice. Many of the top schools make community service part of the acceptance process.

When Marc was taking part in his first-year orientation at Harvard University, he was told by a school administrator that perfect SAT scores did not by any means guarantee acceptance at the university. Many applicants with perfect SAT scores have been rejected over the years because of their narrow concentration on academics. Harvard tremendously values community service and proven leadership skills, and the university will often select a student with a lower SAT score but an active social conscience over a student who has higher test results but has never reached out to the community.

Increasingly, community service is becoming a major component in the selection process of most elite scholarships. One of the four major areas evaluated in the selection process of the prestigious Rhodes Scholarship is service to others.

HELPING OTHERS: GOOD FOR THE BODY

Helping others makes you healthier. Seriously. Physically healthier.

Statistics show that social isolation is a risk factor for a range of health problems.[6] Conversely, volunteering provides people with increased "social contacts and stronger support networks," which make for "lower premature death rates, less heart disease, and fewer health risk factors," according to a government of Canada study.[7] The same study notes: "Some experts have concluded that the health benefits of social relationships may be as important as health risks such as smoking, physical inactivity, and high blood pressure."[8] An Ontario Ministry of Health report found the physical benefits of volunteering to include lowered blood pressure, strengthening of the immune system, and distraction from one's own aches and pains sufficient to increase the efficiency of rehabilitation programs.[9]

Scientific studies have been reporting similar findings for years. A well-known wave of research that began in the mid-1970s has revealed a "dramatic decrease in health problems and death rates for people who are socially involved, compared to those who are isolated,"[10] arguing that social support networks protect against a range of diseases from arthritis and tuberculosis to psychiatric illnesses,[11] and that "people with few social ties had mortality rates two to five times higher than those with more ties."[12] James House, former professor at the University of Michigan, contends that solitary leisure—TV, radio, reading—are insufficient for decreasing stress: it must be human contact.[13]

More recently, Dr. Allan Luks, a researcher at the U.S.-based Institute for the Advancement of Health, concluded that "helping others can truly be one of our most self-serving acts."[14] Luks has made a career out of examining the health benefits of helping others. He popularized the terms "Healthy Helping Phenomenon" (HHP) and "Helper's High" to represent the physical health effects of helping.

The first stage of HHP is a physical high—a rush of good feeling caused by the sudden, powerful release of the body's natural painkillers, the endorphins. It is similar to the high that running and other high-intensity exercise can cause.[15] Phase two of the Healthy Helpers Phenomenon is an equally beneficial sustained calmness, which relieves the distressed body from the cycle of tension, leading to a less taxing use of the body's function and allowing the immune system to restore itself and make the body healthy again.[16]

Luks found that it is the "process of helping, without regard to its outcome, that is the healing factor."[17] Any type of good work will bring benefits! Positive emotions and attitudes—"trust, optimism, and happiness ... are available through the act of helping ... reinforcing feelings of commitment to something worthwhile, thus producing moments of joy and a lasting sense of optimism."[18] Moreover, a critical component of the HHP is a dramatic rise in self-esteem—"the impact of truly feeling needed and of gaining a sense of being accepted in a partnership with other people."[19] Yale professor Lowell Lewin says, "When you're a helper, your self-concept improves. You are somebody. You are worthwhile. And there's nothing more exhilarating than that."[20]

Even *thinking* about helping others can give our health a boost. Psychologist David McClelland of Harvard University had a group of students watch a film about Mother Teresa and her work in the slums of Calcutta. In response to the film, tests on students revealed an increase in immunoglobulin A, an antibody that defends against certain diseases.[21]

Finally, there is the story about the residents of a little town in Pennsylvania called Roseto who caused quite a stir in medical circles. Researchers looked at their mortality records beginning in 1955 and noted that the people of the community had unhealthy lifestyle habits: they reflected a relatively high incidence of alcohol consumption, red meat, and fatty food intake as well as an overall lack of exercise and dieting. But despite all these risk factors, the residents of Roseto had a lower rate of heart attacks than residents of comparable neighboring communities.

The researchers suspected that the distinguishing factor was social support. "The town was known for its close family and community ties and its low levels of social competitiveness." However, while the researchers continued to monitor the town over the years, the "closely-knit mutually supportive social structure" started to disintegrate, and, correspondingly, the good health enjoyed by the majority of its residents began to decline. When community cohesiveness fell apart, the prevalence of heart attacks came to resemble that of the national average.[22] In an age when heart disease continues to be the number one killer in the United States, and 61.8 million American adults suffer from this ailment, perhaps being part of a healthy vibrant community not only gives you a better quality of life—but also a longer life.[23]

A SPECIAL NOTE: HELPING OTHERS—GOOD FOR SENIORS

In Sierra Leone, Free the Children works with a dozen or so religious Sisters who provide secular assistance to the war-ravaged state through development projects. Every time we travel to the country and meet the Sisters, we are amazed at their level of activity. They run the only medical relief operations in the isolated northern regions of the country. Members of the congregation oversee the education of thousands of students in a network of Free the Children schools. They work with women, children, and families in the most desperate of conditions, for long hours, every day. One night, while sitting around the dinner table listening to their moving stories, we respectfully asked the Sisters their ages, and we were totally blown away by their answers. We were anticipating hearing that they were 50 or 55 or so for the most part. To our surprise, we discovered that many were over the age of 75 and some even over the age of 80. But these battle-scarred women looked a fraction of their real ages. They had survived wars, lived in refugee camps with the people they helped, and often went without food for days. But there in the middle of war-torn Sierra Leone, we found the elusive fountain of youth—people dedicated to helping others.

Medical studies among seniors in Canada have linked volunteering to improved quality of life, stronger social networks, increased levels of physical activity, and lower mortality rates. Through reaching out to others and volunteerism, all age groups show a decrease in symptoms of depression; however the greatest benefit is seen in people over the age of 65.[24] Professor Phyllis Moen has found that retired volunteers feel better about themselves—psychologically and physically—than retirees who do not volunteer and older people who still worked and volunteered.[25]

A study by researchers at the University of Michigan followed 423 older married adults for five years to see how giving versus receiving affected longevity. And you guessed it, those who helped others—providing support to friends, relatives, and neighbors and emotional support to their spouses—lived longer. Most amazingly, receiving support had no effect on mortality. The medical community took careful note of these findings, which were published in 2003, because they showed that people live longer *because* they volunteer, not that people volunteer because they are healthier and as a result are more likely to live longer. The researchers also showed that volunteering for less than one hour a week was enough to affect longevity.[26] To be sure, volunteering does a body good!

A SPECIAL NOTE: HELPING OTHERS—GOOD FOR TEENS

Volunteer Now is one of the programs we run in many high schools across North America, and specifically in all 145 public high schools in our hometown, Toronto. It's a fantastic initiative that every year allows tens of thousands of young people to explore their leadership potential by getting out into the community and volunteering—and having fun at the same time. The program introduces service learning, character education, and global citizenship into the school curriculum through the *Take Action!* book series that we have written for students from Grades 6 to 12.[27] What's most amazing is that it is often most successful in alternative schools, which educate students who do not fit into a regular classroom environment. These are often students who are on the verge of dropping out, have been suspended or removed from their regular schools, or are facing serious problems at home. These young people have likely never been told that "they have special talents" or that they can make a positive difference in the lives of others. Volunteering provides them with a constructive outlet for their energy, positive role models, and concrete proof that their contributions can be meaningful to society.

Our experience with the *Volunteer Now* program has shed light on a very important reality: millions of teenagers across North America are so often on the *receiving* end of everything. They receive instructions from adults, homework from teachers, and allowances from their parents. Unfortunately, because of the common assumption that teenagers are at a stage where they have little or nothing to give, people often dismiss the valuable contributions that they can make to others. In doing so, society reinforces feelings of insecurity and low self-esteem so frequently found in this age group.

"I think a lot of people's self-esteem is low because they have never developed a sense of pride in their abilities," notes Dr. Edward Eismann, founder of UNITAS, a community counseling and support agency for young people in the Bronx. Helping others allows you to connect with a variety of people, develop new skills, and prove yourself worthy of someone's trust.[28] We are proud of the remarkable results of the *Volunteer Now* program. School principals in some jurisdictions where it has been implemented report reductions in vandalism and bullying within schools and an increase in school spirit and better teacher morale. Students have found a reason to care—about themselves and others.

Studies show that community service helps a teenager find grounding.[29] In a paper published in *The Journal of Primary Prevention* in 1996, Cynthia W. Moore and Joseph P. Allen show that students who volunteer get better grades and are less likely to drop out of school. The paper also reveals that teens who volunteer are less likely to get pregnant, and they have higher self-esteem and better attitudes toward society.[30]

Between 1991 and 1995, University of Virginia researchers did a study on volunteerism involving 695 students, 85 percent of whom were girls. They found that volunteering provided a boost to self-esteem that affected their lives in many ways. The teens were randomly divided into two groups: one group participated in *Teen Outreach*, a community service program that linked students with volunteer jobs in schools, hospitals, and nursing homes; the second group did no volunteer work. Over the course of four years, the Virginia researchers discovered that 46 percent of the non-volunteer students failed at least one class while only 26 percent of the volunteers failed a course. Among the non-volunteers, nearly 10 percent of the teenage girls became pregnant, compared to 4 percent of the girls who volunteered.[31]

Our work with tens of thousands of young people over the past decade has reinforced in our minds the importance of nurturing a sense of empathy and compassion in young people at an early age. Youths, of course, do not turn 18 and suddenly develop a social conscience. As they become more aware of the world and their place within it, young people come to realize the power they have over their own lives and the lives of others.

THE GREATEST GIFT OF ALL

We have provided you with a slew of statistics (and lots more information in the endnotes), as well as case studies to highlight the benefits of helping others. But even if you did not see practical gains—in the areas of health, business, family and friends, community, and better working environments, you would still have an intangible reward that we believe is the greatest gift of all. Helping others is good for the soul. It provides you with a heightened sense of faith in the world, a reason for hope in your lifetime, and a promise of a brighter future for your children and grandchildren. This is a feeling that buying a new sports car, wearing a new outfit, or striking a huge merger deal cannot give you.

And it is a feeling that you can have every day—not just by volunteering, but by spending a weekend with your children, making ethical shopping choices, and taking action on a social issue. Working for a better world is a positive way to live because at the end of the day, when you are exhausted from working and laughing, you know that you have made a difference. And perhaps that feeling is the greatest gift of all.

My Story

We decided to write our stories together to illustrate how people of different age groups—John is a retired educator and Jordana is a 15-year-old student—can help one another through volunteerism.

JOHN GAITHER

Ahh, those were the days! I was a sprightly 27-year-old, a newly trained teacher with energy and idealism. It was the 1960s and I had just got my Ph.D. I was going to change the world. We all were back then—that and live in a yellow submarine.

Being so young, I got plenty of advice. Teach at an elite private school, they told me. Lecture at a university. Find a job with money and prestige. I didn't listen. Forget money and prestige— I decided to live the simple life with a wife, a child, and a Volvo. I wanted to slog it out in the trenches with the country's battered high school teachers. That was the life for me!

In the end, it really was the life for me. Sure, there were days I regretted my decision. Try teaching a class of Grade 9 or 10 students that learning should be a lifelong experience! But still, I loved the life and I loved the kids—especially the days when a student's eyes lit up as I told stories that related to them and made education—I shudder to use the word—relevant.

The years rushed by. I became the head of my department, then a vice-principal, finally, then a principal—and that's where I stayed. I didn't want to be an administrator. I wanted to be near my students. But, as with every job, the years took their toll. Teaching used to be really enjoyable and being a principal was the reward for being a good teacher, a problem solver, and a community builder. But as education became more politicized, getting up Monday mornings became more difficult. The end of summer came too fast. I grew tired of the budget meetings, the funding cuts, teacher strikes, union lockouts, and work-to-rule. I loved the kids, hated the politics.

I started to dream of retirement. Sitting in traffic on a weekday morning, I would find my mind wandering. I would imagine spending time with my grandchildren, quiet evenings with my wife, traveling, or rediscovering some great books. I told myself that I wouldn't sign myself up for any committees, substitute teaching, or anything requiring a schedule.

I remember my first day of retirement: it was glorious! I cooked a great breakfast for my wife and me, leisurely read the paper, cleaned a bit of the house, and wrote a few letters to friends. On the second day, I cooked a great breakfast, leisurely read the paper...and on the third day, I cooked a great breakfast. ... This is retirement? I tried to tell myself that it was just the transition, that those golden moments were just around the corner, that I would enjoy them soon enough. But something was missing.

A former colleague asked a favor. A group of students were going to Jamaica to work with children in the poorest neighborhoods of Kingston. They were short one chaperone. Would I interrupt my newfound "bliss" and return to the students, just this once? One trip. That's all. My bags were packed and by the door.

The trip was very inspiring. I was moved not only by the poverty I saw but also by the commitment of the young people on the trip and the education they received through this experience. When I returned home I offered to work one day a week with a local youth organization. The experience was so positive that I was soon volunteering nearly full-time, working with students across North America to assist them in becoming involved in their communities and in the world.

Now, it seems, the tables have turned. Some days I am the teacher; others days I am the student. These young people have reawakened my commitment to social justice issues by challenging me to learn more about the situation in the world today, where women and children are exploited and suffer because of corruption, sexism, and greed. Most importantly, they have given me the opportunity to continue to participate in helping to find solutions. In return, I help them administer their charitable projects overseas. I've gone from running one school to helping oversee the construction of schools in 21 countries!

So why do I volunteer? Because it allows me to continue to call upon and to use my skills as a teacher and an administrator working with and for youth in a way I never thought possible in retirement. Volunteering has changed my perception of retirement as the end of a career because I now celebrate it as a new beginning with new challenges and many rewards.

Strange. I'm back working with students, but it doesn't feel like work. Some days, I feel like I am 27 again. I find my spirit renewed every day by the caring young people I meet—people like Jordana Weiss.

JORDANA WEISS

We would have been pals, Emma and I, I'm sure of it. We'd have talked about the books we both loved, tried on hats together, giggled over our funny Buddha collections, and planned how we would someday change the world.

But we never got that chance. Instead, I like to think we're soulmates. It makes me feel as if I will never truly be alone.

Up until my 13th birthday, I'd never heard of Emma Johnstone. It was an important time in my life—my bat mitzvah—and I was having a blast. All my family and friends gathered together to dance, to feast, and to celebrate. But to be honest, I really wasn't into the party—I was more concerned about the presents. See, they weren't for me. I didn't need more jewelry and trinkets. What I really wanted was to build a school in the developing world. I'd asked my guests to bring monetary donations instead.

When the party was over, we sat down and eagerly tallied up the gifts. My guests had been incredibly generous–but we had not raised enough money to build a school. We were only halfway there. Disappointed, I tried to figure out what to do with the money. And that's when I learned about Emma.

Emma lived a three-hour drive away from me, near a lake in the countryside, and from what I hear, she was an amazing girl. Her nickname was the Divine Miss Em. They say she had a sense of the divine about her, an awareness that there's more to this world than what we see. Her teachers liked how she didn't get caught up with the usual silly-girl shenanigans–you know, who's cool, who's not, and who's going out with whom. She liked everybody, and everybody liked her, as I'm sure I would have too. I can tell just by looking at her picture, at the way her laughing eyes seem to leap right out ready to tell me a secret, or something to make me smile.

It seems that everyone in that little town has a story about Emma–how she always brought spare change for the homeless when she visited the big city, how she refused to wear clothes that relied on Third World child labor, how, on her free days, she'd wander over to the nursing home to talk with the old people. And whenever she sent anyone a note or a poem, she'd add this Mother Theresa quote beside her name: "Love never measures. It just gives."

Of course, I didn't know about this back then. All I knew was that thanks to Emma, we were able to build that school after all. It wasn't until later that I got the full story, and when I did, I knew that Emma would always have a special place in my life.

It was a few months before my 13th birthday, and the summer before Emma started eighth grade. Emma's family was in the city waiting nervously for her dad's by-pass operation. She and a friend were sending out e-mails, asking for prayers for him. After working at the computer for awhile they were wilting in the heat so they decided to go for a swim to cool off.

The girls hit the pool that day and, in the blink of an eye—while everyone's thoughts were with her dad—Emma Johnstone simply slipped away.

It was such a small pool, with water only a few feet deep. Who'd have thought there'd be danger there? The girls had been splashing around when the phone rang. When her friend returned from answering the call, she found Emma's lifeless body in the water. It's hard to understand what really happened that day. The inquest later found that Emma didn't do anything stupid or high-risk. She was a competitive swimmer, after all. It seems she just slipped off the ladder and somehow got stuck.

Over the next few days Emma's family lived through shock, anger, and disbelief—a kind of hell known only by people who have been there. Somehow, though, Jan and Gord—Emma's mom and dad—saw through their fog enough to know that Emma would not want people to send flowers. She would want something more "divine." She would want to reach beyond the pain to help others. The Johnstones decided to ask for donations to build a school in a developing country. Emma would have liked that.

The funeral was hugely attended and everyone had a role, from big sister Alex to the pre-teen buddies who wrote the service. And the money poured in.

But it wasn't enough.

John Gaither had been in contact with the Johnstone family and knew how desperately they wanted to build the school in their daughter's name. He also knew how disappointed I was in not raising enough money to build a school.

He asked me if I would like to add my bat mitzvah money to the Johnstones'.

Would I mind? To be able to help poor children and maybe Emma's family too–I was thrilled!

John helped us to find the right location–a small downtrodden village in Ecuador, a cold and foggy outpost where the only schools and hospitals were hours away, where transportation was by foot, the farmland unforgiving, and the children poorly nourished. The new school would be named after Emma. By the following summer it was ready–the Emma Johnstone Escuala– in Llilla, Ecuador. I was invited to join in the official opening.

With a lump in my throat and butterflies in my stomach, I made the long journey south, first by plane, then by truck, and finally by horseback. The whole way I carried a picture of Emma, a photo her dad had taken in the sunshine of her yard, a smiling girl with eyes that won't stay put. I carried Emma's picture along a rocky path to the top of one of the world's tallest mountains, to a cluster of thatched huts, to the arms of the colorfully dressed villagers huddled in the clouds.

It was there, so close to the heavens, that Emma's soul, and her school, were blessed. As the village children sang softly in their native voice, their leader sprinkled a mixture of incense, herbs, and tobacco into a metal pan filled with burning coal. Fragrant black smoke wafted up and around us. The leader spoke of Emma's goodness and her generosity. With her words, the smoke became Emma's spirit. She waved the smoke over three tiny pine tree seedlings–one for Emma, one for me and the other volunteers, and one for Llilla's new school. She circled the smoking pan over the trees as they were placed in the ground near the school, gathering Emma's spirit to its heart. She bade Emma to watch over the children there. Then she asked me to bless the remaining incense and to return it to Emma's parents.

I watched the smoke drift northward, twining in the soft breeze like a rope binding us all together—Emma, the Ecuadoreans, and me. I realized that no matter where we live, we can all understand tragedy, feel others' pain and hunger, and want to help.

When I returned home, my family drove across the rolling farmland to meet Emma's parents and deliver the incense from the ceremony. Pulling into the driveway of Emma's tiny old house by the lake, I was struck by how different her life had been from mine—and yet, in many ways the same. Emma's dog trotted across the yard to greet us—the same color and breed as mine back home. In her bedroom under the eaves, I found Emma's collection of hats, books, and buddhas, eerily similar to mine.

But those were superficial similarities. There was something more. Emma's parents called it an "essence" that used to shine from Emma's face, which they could see shining from my face now. They told me that, and I could feel my eyes fill with tears, the same tears I saw in theirs.

It has been two years since my bat mitzvah. I believe that souls that are alike are attracted to each other. I believe that Emma's soul found mine, teaching me that, though our bodies will not be here forever, our actions will, and the lives we touch today ensure that our own lives carry on. Emma and I were strangers once; we are soulmates now. Together, we have been able to do great things.

Chapter 10:

HELP YOURSELF TO A BETTER WORLD: JOIN THE MOVEMENT

"Never doubt that a small group of thoughtful, committed citizens can change the world. Indeed, it's the only thing that ever has."
– Margaret Mead –
(1901–1978)
Anthropologist

If reaching out and helping others is so beneficial for us socially, emotionally, mentally, and physically, then why aren't all people doing it? Why don't we have a world full of interactive and cooperative communities, in which everybody gets along, helps one another, and feels good?

Well, first, our society's tragic underconsumption of broccoli appears to indicate that we haven't yet arrived at that stage of evolution where we all do what's good for our health.

Second, we're stuck. In Grade 10 science class, we called it "inertia": the tendency of a body to remain in a uniform, perpetual state of rest or motion until acted upon by an external force. Millions of us are bystanders on a massive, worldwide scale. We know there are problems. We know people need help. We know we *can* help. But most of us continue to stand by.

Moving beyond our societal inertia won't be easy. The problems we see every day in the media are often intimidating because of their sheer size and complexity, and our self-help culture makes it difficult for us to even care. We feel paralyzed by the conflicting choices that we *think* we have to make between what is popular and what is right. Often without real grounds, we fear that others will see us as "abnormal" or "radical" if we begin to question the injustices around us.[1] What will happen if we stand out from the crowd and no one follows? What will happen if we don't succeed?

Those same risks stood before women seeking equality with men, African Americans seeking civil rights, South Africans seeking an end to apartheid, countless peoples around the world (including Americans) seeking self-determination and independence from colonialism, and peace activists seeking a ban on the use of landmines. The realities they faced were different from their vision of a better world. Colossal barriers lined their path to a just society. Inertia appeared overwhelming. But it was *not* insurmountable.

The precise reasons for the success of the world's most celebrated social movements are hotly debated in academic literature and activist circles. But their beginnings are uncontestable: somebody *did* something. A bystander acted. Inertia was pushed into action.

THE MOVEMENT FROM *ME TO WE*

Our world has experienced profound challenges in the last few years: the bursting of the dot-com bubble, corporate scandals, the tragic events of September 11, the wars in Afghanistan and Iraq. At this critical juncture in human history, where isolationism and the self-help culture have come to dominate our society, and where millions of people are searching for more, we believe that we need a new social movement of people who think and act in the mindset of "We" so that we all benefit, both collectively and personally. This movement is characterized by a spirit of compassion and justice, where we look out for not only our own individual interests, but also those of others—people in our local and global communities, our environment, our families, and ourselves.

When people think of movements, they immediately envision marches and demonstrations, public protests, petitions, and the changing of laws. While these activities are elements of a social movement, they are not its end goal. The Movement Action Plan, a theory of and guide to social movements developed by renowned activist Bill Moyer, defines social movements as "collective actions in which the populace is alerted, educated, and mobilized, sometimes over years and decades, to challenge the powerholders and the whole society to redress social problems or grievances and restore critical social values."[2] A movement is thus built upon values, and its goal is to bring about a fundamental shift in the psyche of a people.

In writing this book, we, too, are seeking a shift in the social psyche, in how individuals think about themselves and others. The movement from *Me to We* means living our lives as socially conscious and responsible citizens, engaging in daily acts of compassion and kindness, building meaningful relationships and community, and considering the impact on *We* when making decisions in our own lives. It challenges us to see ourselves as part of a greater entity and to live with the realization that all our actions or inactions affect not only us, but also others in our evolving world. This may not seem as dramatic as the social movements of the past. These acts will probably not capture the front page of the paper. But the end result will be just as powerful and important—a shift in the thinking of people, their values, beliefs, attitudes, and, yes, daily decisions. As we go from being detached spectators to active participants in our community, we move from *Me to We* with the understanding that we are all interconnected and that helping others is better for us all.

We may not reach the end of this thousand-mile journey in our lifetime, but as Lao Tzu said, one has to take the first step.

We know that each and every positive step makes the world a better place. Furthermore, as historian and activist Howard Zinn argues, "the reward for participating in a movement for social justice is not the prospect of future victory. It is the exhilaration of standing together with other people, taking risks together, enjoying small triumphs and enduring disheartening setbacks–together."[3]

Yes, we are idealists. Yes, the world we envision seems difficult to achieve. Yes, we realize that we have a lot of people to convince. But sometimes it takes a little bit of idealism to change the world.

Women voting? Yeah right, Harriet Taylor.[4] An end to slavery? Surely you jest, Frederick Douglass.[5] An international ban on landmines? Get out of town, Jody Williams.[6] A black president of South Africa? Nelson Mandela[7], you are too much!

When studying the history of social movements, we remember major events like the Storming of the Bastille during the French Revolution, the "March on Washington" when Martin Luther King gave his impassioned "I Have a Dream" speech, or the Rivonia Trial when Nelson Mandela was sentenced to life imprisonment. But we usually overlook the smaller, daily actions and sacrifices of thousands of ordinary people that provided the foundation for these social movements to become a reality.

The civil rights movement was fueled by the actions of individuals like Rosa Parks, who in 1955 refused to move to the back of the bus in her hometown of Montgomery, Alabama. This small action sent forth a ripple and grew into a wave that spread to the hearts of millions of people prompting them to speak about the issue in fields and factories, on their front porches and around kitchen tables, in town halls and churches. Small groups of people came together, discussed and debated, struggled and strived, organized and spoke out. They lived through pain, setbacks, abuse, and distress before a single civil rights marcher ever placed a foot on the Washington Monument. Every action taken by an individual and group to stand up against segregation and systemic discrimination contributed to the successes of the movement, the work of which is still not finished, but has profoundly altered the course of American history.[8]

A wave of small, daily, individual actions also lay at the heart of the movement for women's rights. In July of 1848, Elizabeth Cady Stanton, a young wife and mother living in upstate New York, sat in her parlor with four women friends enjoying afternoon tea. She lamented the fact that the American Revolution, which was fought to put an end to tyranny, had not gone far enough. The rights of women were still not being adequately protected, even though women had played an integral role in ensuring the success of the war. The others present strongly agreed with her observations. These five women were not the first group to have such discussions; however, they were one of the first to decide to take decisive action, leading the call for the first ever women's rights convention in 1848. Years later, Alice Paul, a famous women's rights organizer and the author of the Equal Rights Amendment that was passed in 1923, commented, "I always feel the movement is sort of a mosaic. Each of us puts in one little stone, and then you get a great mosaic."[9]

Social movements like the civil rights and women's movements are not just for the history books. Struggles continue today over these issues and others, including aboriginal issues, disability rights, poverty and hunger, the environment, and numerous other global problems. They have been built on the actions and energy of thousands of individuals and groups striving to create a better world, step by step.

We have seen the power of social movements to bring about change. Free The Children is an example of what a small group of ordinary people—even children—can do when they are willing to take that first most important step to help another.

Ten years ago, we would have laughed if someone had told us that the Free the Children would grow to be so large today, having already affected the lives of over one million children worldwide. We started with small actions–giving speeches in local schools, a neighborhood garage sale to raise money to improve the lives of poor children, and a petition to call for more government intervention to protect children's rights.

Having discovered that education is one of the best solutions to ending the exploitation of children, our first development project was raising money to build a one-room schoolhouse in Nicaragua to provide education to 40 children. This initial step was the hardest! We had so much to learn, cynics told us that we would never succeed, and we even doubted our own abilities. However, after our first success, each action became a little easier. We set a goal of building 10 schools, then 50, then 100, then 250–and, over the years, we surpassed these milestones and have built over 400 primary schools in 21 nations, providing daily education to more than 35,000 children, and giving them the opportunity to break the cycle of illiteracy and poverty. All of these projects were built on the foundation of that first school– that first action and now hundreds of thousands of young people in North America and around the world have joined this movement of "children helping children."

SETTING THE STAGE FOR A SOCIAL MOVEMENT

The key to this success was three-fold. First, we were willing to take a risk. By taking a stand, we put ourselves "on the line" and faced the possibility of failure. When Craig stood up in front of his Grade 7 class and spoke about the article that had inspired him regarding the young boy sold into child labor, he took a risk. There was a risk that he would be laughed at by his peers. There was a risk that no one would join him.

There was a risk that no one would care. But he decided to speak up anyway. It wasn't that he was without anxiety—in fact, he was incredibly nervous! But he was able to overcome his fear because this story had touched him so deeply, and because he was so firm in his belief that he had to act.

We were nervous the first time we challenged an adult on a social justice issue. We were uneasy the first time we asked someone for a donation. We were scared when we first boarded a plane to travel to Asia and leave behind the friends and family whom we had come to rely upon throughout our childhood. It was difficult for us to take these first steps. And it may be equally difficult for you to take your first step—whether it be reaching out to a neighbor in need, walking into a hospital to volunteer, or stepping outside your comfort zone and taking action on an issue that is important to your community. But that first step is critical. Once the inertia is broken, each act builds upon the foundation of the previous one, and each step becomes a little easier. In the same way, every social movement has its setbacks and triumphs. Although standing up for what you value is not an easy task, it can be a very rewarding one. Borrowing from the thoughts of Rabbi Hillel: We get up. We walk. We fall down and get up again. Meanwhile we keep dancing. We do not want to miss the joy of it all.

The second reason for the success of Free the Children is that we were not alone in this journey. The organization grew beyond our initial vision and became a movement shared by many people—especially children who realized that they, too, had power to change the world.

In taking the first step you may feel alone—we certainly felt that way when we started. However, people quickly began to take note of our activities and offered to help. Support first came from the individuals who were closest to us: our parents and our family members. Then our energy and passion became contagious and our friends and classmates began to help. Then our friends' friends did as well. The organization grew by word of mouth, and we soon began to receive e-mails from complete strangers who had heard about the movement and wanted to be of assistance.

Being among the initial members of any movement requires a leap of faith. Although you will see the immediate result of your actions through smiles and expressions of gratitude, you may not see their full impact for years, or may possibly never even know how deeply you touched the life of another person.

We knew that Free the Children chapters were springing up around the world, even in schools in remote towns in the United States and Canada, and in countries like Japan and Brazil. But it was only years later that we learned that dozens of other youth organizations were formed by young people who had been inspired by the story of Free the Children. Over the last ten years, we have received thousands of letters from young people who were motivated to engage in individual actions to help others, and countless phone calls from teachers and parents who tell us that Free the Children helped their students and children find direction in their lives.

While you may never actually see the others who are taking action at the same time, you must have faith that they, like you, are quietly working for a better world. Rosa Parks had faith that people would follow her example and sit in the front of public buses across America as an act of defiance against injustice. Martin Luther King had faith that people would march with him in towns and cities across the United States in order to break down the barriers of prejudice. Nelson Mandela had faith that people in South Africa would stand up with him against discrimination. As Martin Luther King once said: "Take the first step in faith. You don't have to see the whole staircase, just take the first step."

The third and perhaps most important reason for the success of Free the Children is also arguably the most simple: it was a movement whose time had come. Previously, organizations espousing children's issues had worked *for* children, but rarely *with* children, denying young people a voice in decisions that affected their future. Can you imagine a conference on women's rights that excluded women? The idea of a network of children helping children was part of the growth of a larger movement that recognized the valuable contributions that young people could make in helping themselves and their peers.

Importantly, Free the Children was able to leverage the Internet, an inexpensive system of communication, to connect children from around the world. One e-mail could reach hundreds of thousands of students in schools across the continents. For the first time in history, children from around the globe were able to stand up together, in solidarity, for their own rights and the rights of their peers in developing countries.

Social movements–a pivotal change in thinking–wait for the right set of circumstances to be present before they emerge. People involved in mediation in conflict areas have told us that only when both sides accept the fact that their current situation is causing them pain and recognize that neither side can change the situation alone–something they called "a hurting stalemate"[10]–are they willing to move ahead. The question is whether we as a society have reached the stage where people feel unfulfilled, frustrated, and unhappy enough to willingly make a change in their own lives. This is the point of impasse from which all movements begin. For generations, people knew that slavery was wrong, that African Americans and women should have the right to vote, and that apartheid was evil. However, there finally came a time when social, political, and economic factors made the women's rights, civil rights, and anti-apartheid movements possible. This hurting stalemate, an inner readiness for change, is the first stage in the emergence of a social movement. The second stage is the trigger that sets it in motion.

In his well-known book, *Tipping Point*, Malcolm Gladwell argues that large-scale changes in societal attitudes and behaviors are like epidemics. The slightest action or change in environment has the power to tip society's attitude and behavior with respect to an issue. Either through the extraordinary actions of a few people, the overwhelming persuasiveness of a message or idea, or an unrelated change in the overall environment, a widespread social trend can sweep into existence: the result is that inertia is blown off the map. The message behind the *Tipping Point* is that *any* small action can be the one to tip a situation into what becomes a far-reaching phenomenon. And, more importantly, every small action that is taken contributes to creating the perfect environment for the tipping point to occur.

The *Me to We* philosophy is an idea whose time has come. It is the alternative for which we have been searching, and the foundation of a happier, more compassionate, and more fulfilling community for all of us. To participate in the movement from *Me to We*, you have to be willing to take action, however small, to improve the life of another. You do not have to start with a major world problem. As hard as it might seem to believe, your one letter, one dollar, one smile, or one act could be the tipping point—if not of the entire movement, then the tipping point in the life of one person. You may never know how many others are engaging in similar actions, but you will not be alone. You can only begin to imagine the ripples you send forward as others are inspired to join you in this movement.

What we often forget about Grade 10 science is that inertia *also* refers to the capacity of an entity to move relentlessly forward forever. All it takes is one small force—one tipping point—to give it a push, and it will carry itself forth into eternity.

My Story

LINDSAY AVNER

I knew what it meant. Mom was going to die.

I was 11 years old. Mom was sitting at the kitchen table, staring down at her cup of tea, running her fingers round the rim. It took her a few seconds to look up. I'd never seen that kind of look on her face before.

For as long as I can remember, breast cancer had stalked our family. Grandma died of it at the age of 39, Great-grandma passed away from the same disease. Several aunts on both my mom's and dad's side died of breast cancer, too. There were no females left now, except Mom and me.

And now it had snared my mom, too.

From this day on, I thought to myself, *there will never be another day where things will be happy and okay.*

That's pretty much how it was.

I'd come home from school to find my mom throwing up in a bucket in her room, the house a mess, and no dinner in sight. I'd drop my backpack—and childhood—at the door and take over as surrogate mom. Me—who'd never willingly touched a vacuum in my life—cleaning house, doing laundry, bathing and reading to my little brother Jory. Dad tried to help, but he had to work late to pay the medical bills and keep the family afloat, so it was up to me.

One day, it was all too much. Instead of heading out for recess, I stood in the girls' washroom and cried. Through blurry eyes, I could see a classmate approach. "You know, Lindsay," the girl said in that catty pre-teen way, "you can't just blame everything on your mom's cancer." With a toss of her hair she walked away.

That's when I crumbled. *No one understands!* I wept quietly to myself. *I'm watching my mom's hair fall out, watching her die!* I had never felt so alone.

The worst was the moment of fake hope, when the doctors told us the cancer was gone. Mom was going to be okay! We were going to be happy again! Mom started exercising, eating right, her hair started to grow back. I struggled to get my own life back to normal.

Then the cancer came back. Ovarian cancer, this time—a basketball-sized growth that had to be removed immediately. Mom was rushed to New York for surgery. *This can't be happening!* I was reeling. *This is so unfair!*

The chemo, the nausea, and the fear—it all came back again. "You've got to be strong," people said to me. "Gotta be strong for Jory. Gotta get through this."

Somehow, Mom made it. The doctors said it was a miracle: she beat cancer a second time. They were thrilled. It was time to make that slow climb back to normal. But not me. It was too late. *You want me to be happy again, just like that?* Nope. Not happening. I was bitter and tired and angry. The cancer was in my family, probably in me too and would eventually strike. It took my childhood, probably my future. I was a mess. When I wasn't in my room crying, I was thundering about the house, or moping with another friend who was upset over her parents' divorce. We had nothing in common except our sadness, so we sat and sulked.

"Come on, run with me." Mom was on my back again. She wanted me to run in the marathon for the local breast cancer fundraiser. Thought it'd be good for me. It would get me out of the house. I didn't want to go. I wanted to wallow.

But she kept at it, kept hammering away. All right then. Fine. I'll go. Just this once. To make her happy, I signed up for Run for the Cure.

Tying my shoes on the day of the race, I snuck a peek around. I saw old people, young children, women, and men. No one I knew. No one my age. I started to question why I was here. The gun blasted and the race was on. Through the blur I caught a glimpse of words on T-shirts: "I run for the memory of my sister," "I run for the memory of my Gran." I didn't want to see that. I looked to the sidelines where well-wishers handed out water bottles. "Only two more miles!" they cheered. "You can do it." Right. *What if I don't want to do it?* I turned up my Walkman and ran faster, watching my shoes flashing white on the road. I felt a stitch in my side, a nagging ache. *Maybe I should quit?*

And there it was—the finish line. Gulping for air, I lifted my face up to the sky, felt my aching muscles and my hammering heart. I felt good. I felt strangely energized. I think I even started to smile—but I swallowed it, quickly, when I saw who was behind me. There, approaching the finish line was *me*—Lindsay—a little girl with freckle-speckled cheeks and dark curly hair. The little girl was the spitting image of me when I was small. And across her tiny T-shirt, the black printed words: "*I run for the memory of my mom.*"

Suddenly, I couldn't breathe. Standing in the middle of the cheering crowd, I realized that little girl could have been me! My mom was still alive, and I couldn't imagine life without her. I rose on tiptoe, scanned the crowd to find her. I wanted to run to my mother, to hold her tight.

Things were different after that. I saw that I wasn't alone, and I saw that there was hope, and courage, and companionship if I just reached out. *That's it,* I vowed, *I'm getting off my butt and taking charge of my life!*

I decided to organize the first Race for the Cure–High School Challenge. My friends were skeptical at first. But like my mom, I kept plugging away until I won them over. More than 350 teens showed up at that first race–way more than I'd ever dreamed. It was amazing: everyone pouring praise on me, strangers writing letters, confiding in me. Who'd have thought? Within two years, it grew to 15 different races around the country, from New Jersey to Hollywood, with 11 schools in Los Angeles alone.

And me? I'm running regularly now. It's made me stronger, more able to help my mom should she need me again, more able to fight cancer myself should it ever dare to ambush me. I'm planning a career in breast cancer advocacy. And I'm telling everyone I know that you just have to keep on trying. Everyone goes through bad times. It's not easy. You have to pick yourself up and keep on going. I know I'll keep going, keep running–for myself, for my mom, and for the cure.

Chapter 11:

BE THE CHANGE
YOU WANT TO SEE

*"When we are dreaming alone, it is only a dream. But when
we are dreaming together, it is the beginning of reality."*
– Don Helder Camara –
(1909–1999)
Bishop

We once attended an international youth conference where
thousands of young people had gathered to learn about the
challenges facing our world and to brainstorm possible solutions. By the last day, we all felt inspired by what we had
learned, but also concerned that our action plans would be too
small to overcome the world's enormous problems–that they
wouldn't even make a dent.

All the participants gathered in the hushed stadium for the
closing ceremonies of the conference. One young person stood
in the center of the facility, holding a lit candle, and called out
the one question that was on all our minds:

"I am one person. What difference can I make?"

She then turned to the four people closest to her and lit the
candles in their hands. Those four walked out to the corners of
the stadium, repeated the question, and each lit the candles of
four people they met there. The same question was echoed by
the group several times and, on each occasion, the flame was
passed forward. In this way, the firelight spread from one person

to thousands, until finally, every candle was lit, and the whole stadium was aglow.

It was a simple, but powerful statement. While it may seem naïve, it's important to recognize that every major social change comes about in this way, through very small, simple actions that spread like wildfire.

We can begin the movement from *Me to We* by taking small or large actions in our home, in our workplace, within our faith group, within our community, and among all of us, including our young people. The key to the equation is *action*—making decisions and acting in the mindset of "We."

BEGINNING AT HOME

"The word 'family' implies warmth, a place where the core feelings of the heart are nurtured."
– Doc Childre and Howard Martin –

A better world begins at home. The *Me to We* movement can take root in simple actions that we do every day among the people dear to us. If we don't like the direction in which society is moving, we have to recognize that we are setting its course with the lessons we teach our children. Society is something that we create, and we have the ability to change it.

In our personal experience, our mother wanted to give us every opportunity in the world, but she did not over-schedule us with practices for sports teams or clubs. She thought that it was also important for us to learn about the world and to develop a social conscience. She helped us to believe that we could do something about the situations around us, from a classmate who was being bullied at school, to the images of poverty we saw on the evening news. Spending time together as a family, whether in formal or informal volunteer settings, was an important part of our childhood. It was where we met with friends and learned more about life than we ever could from textbooks.

When we wanted to do something and were faced with uncertainty or fear of taking the first step, our mother would encourage us, telling us that "The only failure is not trying." Even once all the safety precautions were in place, she still went against all her motherly instincts and allowed us to leave home at an early age to travel and volunteer in developing countries, and to learn more about the world. This was the beginning of some phenomenal life-changing experiences for us.

Our greatest memories are of time spent together as a family, being involved in our larger community. For example, growing up, we went on camping trips with our father and other families in the community arranged through a local service organization. Dad would cook in the camps with the other fathers during the day as we ran off adventuring with our friends. In the evenings, we'd all come together around the campfire, roast marshmallows, and listen to the fathers tell ghost stories. Several times, we stuck around for a few extra days and went on fishing trips, just our dad and the two of us. These are some of the fondest memories we have of our father. We were both still young, and to be honest, if Dad had suggested the fishing trip when we were just sitting around at home, we would have said, "No way!" (It just wasn't a cool thing to do, we thought.) But when he came out and volunteered at the camp, we ended up spending a lot of great time together, and it just seemed natural to go off on our own afterwards and keep having fun.

How can the *Me to We* philosophy become a part of your own family's lives? Some suggestions might be to schedule specific nights during the week when the whole family has dinner together with the television off. (Make this as much of a priority as the 9 a.m. staff meeting.) Spend time volunteering as a family at a local food bank or a soup kitchen; a group home for the handicapped; an immigration center helping new immigrants to learn English; a conservation area; a local arts, music, or historical society, or political campaign center. We can guarantee that this will bring your family closer together. Discuss current events and important social issues and what you can do to help. Have fun together! Go hiking, bike riding, or jogging. Create greater intergenerational connections; children can interview their grandparents about their early lives and they can make a book about it together or research their family tree. The list goes on... If families turned the television off more often and spent time together, not only would we have stronger family bonds, but also more vital communities.

IN THE WORKPLACE

The 2003 *Maclean's* magazine "Best Companies to Work For" list found that when employees are given the opportunity to meet informally and volunteer together, staff morale and productivity shoot way up.[1] The company Direct Energy links its charitable giving to the number of volunteer hours put in by its employees; it makes donations to the organizations where they volunteer, thus supporting its employees and the community at the same time. Other companies distribute awards to celebrate staff members who are socially involved, and designate service days where workers can spend time, alongside senior management, taking part in true team-building activities by volunteering together. Wells Fargo gives personal growth leaves. Xerox allows social service sabbaticals. The Body Shop gives employees a half-day off per week with pay to engage in volunteer activities. Many companies permit job sharing[2] to facilitate more time with family and community, including Hewlett-Packard, Black and Decker, TRW Vidar, and Levi-Strauss.[3] The *Me to We* movement is very much evident in these companies, and their example could certainly be emulated in other workplaces.

Businesses often donate their products or services to organizations serving the community. One remarkable story is that of Lekha Singh, an individual who pioneered a non-profit application of technology that was first developed by a for-profit company. She founded a Dallas, Texas-based organization called Aidmatrix, which provides the software link between corporations that have excess products to donate and charities that can put the products to use.[4]

Incorporating the *Me to We* philosophy into the workplace is a question of daily choices and actions. Look for a need and respond to it, and make decisions that consider the perspectives of other people. This is what Art DeFehr did, when as CEO of Canada's largest assembled-furniture manufacturer, employing more than 5,000 people, he was offered the option of moving his company's headquarters away from Winnipeg, Manitoba, where it was founded, in order to take advantage of lower taxes elsewhere. He declined the move, against the advice of his accountants and business manager, preferring to stay loyal to his community. "I *could* pay less tax..." he conceded, but that would hurt the community that had always supported the company and was home to 90 percent of his staff. "We have made the decision that we'll pay taxes where we live and work," he said.[5]

In what other ways can the *Me to We* philosophy take root in the workplace? Some suggestions might include becoming genuinely interested in the people you work with not only as colleagues, but also as friends; inviting someone sitting alone to join you for lunch; or celebrating special events and the accomplishments of team members. Technology can be used for connecting with others by posting a calendar of volunteer events, e-mailing out action campaigns to your co-workers, or electronically organizing the office staff to participate in fundraisers, such as dress-down days or walk-a-thons. You can invite social service organizations in the community to come to the workplace and speak about available volunteer opportunities. Companies can also use their professional skills to do pro bono work in the community, arrange for a percentage of your monthly paycheck to be automatically designated as a charitable donation, and ensure that their business and personal ethics are always aligned.

IN YOUR COMMUNITY

Do you make a point of getting to know your neighbors? Or the people who work in the businesses and shops in your area? One of the best ways to build these links and friendships is by joining or starting a community association. By building community associations, we create the connections that allow us to share our common concerns, and to work and live together in a more caring environment, giving rise to the movement from *Me to We*. After visiting the United States in 1831, French statesman Alexis de Tocqueville observed in his famous work, *Democracy in America*:

> I have always admired the extreme skill with which the inhabitants of the United States succeeded in proposing a common object for the exertions of a great many men and in inducing them voluntarily to pursue it.[6]

Generations have passed since this observation was made; however, we can work to mend our torn social fabric by coming together to support our communities. All it takes is a small group of people to effect change in a neighborhood, start a local clean-up initiative, or challenge a questionable development project. Working together to address common problems shows us that we are not alone and empowers all individuals involved. It is a way to rekindle the feeling of connectedness to others, celebrate our accomplishments, and strengthen our nation, community by community.

To learn more about what motivates community action, we sat down with June Callwood, a Canadian legend for her charitable work and social advocacy for the poor, the homeless, and children's rights. The author of 28 books, she also made time to found or co-found over 50 social action organizations, including an AIDS hospice, a youth hostel, a hostel for women, a center for teenage parents, and a civil liberties foundation. At 80 years of age, and recently diagnosed with terminal cancer, she zooms around Toronto in a little red sports car, which she showed us with a smile and a laugh. And after more than 50 years of public commitment, she still has a sparkle in her eyes and radiates hope. We were eager to discover the source of her dedication to others.

"What motivated you to become involved in social issues?" we asked.

"I did it because it was the right thing to do," she said.

"But your whole life has been devoted to helping others. Was it because of your faith, a personal philosophy you hold dear, or some sudden tragedy in your life?" (Casey House, a well-known Toronto hospice for people dying from AIDS was initiated by June, and named after her son, who was killed at the age of 20 by a drunk driver.)

"No," she responded, "only because there was a need and it was the right thing to do. No other reason."

June must have sensed our frustration in trying to discover her source of inspiration and commitment. She went on to explain to us that she had grown up in a small town, Belle River, not far from the Detroit-Windsor border, and her approach to life had been largely shaped by her family and upbringing. Belle

River was a place where people took care of one another, she told us. When someone was sick or was having a tough time, neighbors would bring food. When there was an accident or a death, people were there to help and to offer support. Neighbors looked out for one another's children. Farmers supported each other in difficult times. In this tight-knit community, people were neighborly and helped one another.

When June moved to Toronto, however, she was shocked to see the overwhelming presence of hunger, homelessness, and pain in the city—and to find so few people responding. Founding a shelter for abused women, working to help victims of AIDS, or fighting to improve the situation of the homeless was simply an extension of what she had learned as a child— that a community is like a big family and "taking care of each other is the right thing to do." June's explanation for her activism brought to mind Martin Luther King Jr.'s words:

> Cowardice asks the question, 'Is it safe?' Expediency asks the question, 'Is it politic?' Vanity asks the question, 'Is it popular?' But, conscience asks the question, 'Is it right?' And there comes a time when one must take a position that is neither safe, nor politic, nor popular, but one must take it because one's conscience tells one that it is right."

There are countless ways to launch the movement from *Me to We* in your community. Possibly, you are reading this book because you belong to a book club that comes together once a month to choose a book to read, and then discuss its message. One suggestion might be to use the book club model to start a "*Me to We* Club," in which you and a group of friends meet once a month and "adopt an action." The action can be as simple as making a conscious effort to indulge in simple gestures like holding doors open for people, being a courteous driver, and greeting people with a friendly smile. Some groups personally welcome newcomers into the area, organize their communities to participate in a car-free day, a clean-up event, or a neighborhood garage sale for a charitable cause.

You can choose to volunteer at the local library, animal shelter, or hospital, or join the parent-teacher council at your child's school. People are always needed to hand out brochures and man the telephones to promote a community fundraiser or, instead of founding a new club, as an individual, you can participate in a political campaign or circulate a petition on an issue you care about. You might choose something more complex, such as becoming part of a group that campaigns to help work in international development to promote education, women's rights, or tackle health issues such as AIDS.

Imagine the potential of bringing this model to other service clubs or religious groups in your community and challenging them to take action on a common issue, or encouraging entire cities to adopt specific actions to build greater community spirit. Imagine how many people could be inspired and rallied to one cause, and the incredible force that would create.

True to the essence of its philosophy, spreading the message of *Me to We* among friends and community members helps both others and yourself at the same time. Many people fail to follow typical self-help programs because they lack a coach or a friend to help keep them focused on their goals. This approach is like having a buddy who gets you out of bed in the morning to go for a jog—sometimes you need that extra boost. Spreading the message to friends or starting your own group with regular meetings and routines helps you create a strong support network for living the message. Phyllis Moen, a professor in Life Course Studies in human development and sociology at the University of Minnesota, states that among those who volunteer, 44 percent do so because they were asked. By reaching out to others, the movement from *Me to We* takes root in your community, and the power of one becomes the power of many.

IN YOUR FAITH GROUP

There is a memorable story about the time Mother Teresa traveled to the Middle East and was stopped at a border crossing by a guard. "Are you carrying any weapons?" he asked. "Yes I am," she answered. Taken aback, the security guard asked her to show him her weapons. Mother Teresa opened her bag and pulled out her prayer books and notes. "These are my weapons," she answered, "my prayers and my good deeds with people." These were her weapons for fighting hunger, loneliness, sickness, and discord. Mother Teresa believed that service to others was an essential part of living her faith. She had found happiness and meaning in her relationship with God and with the many people in her life.

The *Me to We* movement has a natural home among religious groups and organizations. One of the greatest rewards of helping others is finding purpose and meaning in our lives, something that is integral to our personal understanding of faith. Helping others leads us to rediscover our connection to the world, and that may be in a spiritual or religious sense. During our visits to countries such as the Philippines and Nicaragua, we are always amazed by the actions taken by faith-based organizations that have come together to provide assistance to the local population. From the slums of Manila to the mountains of Waslala, the religious groups that we visited were running soup kitchens, shelters for street children, and support groups for battered women. In these countries, practicing one's faith involves much more than simply attending a religious service. It means actively living the message to create community and networks of mutual support.

In an age when many people question their faith, charitable work can provide new hope and a reason to believe. One often reads stories of people whose charitable deeds are motivated by their religious beliefs: Jimmy Carter and the Aga Khan come immediately to mind. For the two of us, it was the opposite. While we have always been religious, we found the true meaning of our faith through service to others.

Some people ask us how we maintain our hope when confronted with overwhelming sights of human deprivation, the scourge of AIDS, and the devastation of war. We respond by saying that in the midst of such horrendous human suffering, we often find the greatest virtue and human potential. We have met many extraordinary men and women who give selflessly of themselves. We have seen teachers spending their own money to help at-risk students in America's urban centers, aid workers toiling to the point of exhaustion to care for desperate people in refugee camps, and mediators risking their lives to secure peace in the middle of war zones. Witnessing extraordinary acts of passion and courage stirs the deepest faith within one's soul— even individuals not motivated by religious beliefs are filled with a renewed faith in humanity, a conviction that the world can be a better place, and that hope is a worthy ideal.

How can the *Me to We* philosophy take root in religious organizations? One suggestion is through greater inter-faith coalitions. When Marc was volunteering in Thailand, he worked under the auspices of an American priest whose organization brought secular assistance to the slum community. Marc was constantly amazed at how the volunteers of various religious persuasions, whether they were Catholic, Protestant, Jewish, Muslim, or Buddhist, all worked side by side for the common purpose of helping those in need. When people of different faiths work together, they are united by their similarities and can celebrate their differences. It is possible to reach the ideal echoed by Martin Luther King, who longed for the day "when all of God's children, black men and white men, Jews and Gentiles, Protestants and Catholics, will be able to join hands..." Joint actions of religious groups might include campaigns to improve their neighborhoods, tackling issues such as racism or youth violence, taking part in activities to help the homeless members of the community or the elderly who live alone, or participating in social action campaigns to help support initiatives like Jubilee 2000.[7] Faith groups might also consider organizing a service committee, asking members to adopt a specific action, and discussing volunteer initiatives among their congregations.

ENGAGING YOUNG PEOPLE

*"The future belongs to those who believe
in the beauty of their dreams."*
− Eleanor Roosevelt −
(1884–1952)
Diplomat, former First Lady of the United States

Young people have been, and increasingly are, at the forefront of many social justice movements, including the anti-apartheid movement in South Africa, the worldwide environmental movement, the American civil rights movement, and the '60s peace movement that germinated on college campuses across North America. Today, because of media and technology, children and youth are more aware of social, environmental, and political issues than ever before. However, our culture still views youths as "adults in waiting." Young people need to recognize that they are not only called upon to be the leaders of tomorrow–they must also be the leaders of *today*–in their communities and their world. They may not be able to vote, but they can bring about change, as they have strong and determined voices, limitless energy and enthusiasm, and a firm belief that much of their ideal world is within reach.

Adults can nurture the development of this new *We* generation of youth in many ways. Support and encourage the young people in your life to become active members of their community helping others, volunteering, and participating in social issues. All groups have a role in this process. Families can foster a sense of compassion from the earliest years; schools can support character education and service learning initiatives; and faith groups can establish volunteer programs to help youths live their beliefs. Young people should be encouraged to discuss the issues and problems that surround them, rather than be sheltered from the "big, bad world" (trust us, they already know about it). Discourage apathy and 24/7 television and Internet, and support real-life learning and active citizenship.

Finally, it is important for adults to live the message *by modeling the behaviors they wish to see in young people.* Reach out. Volunteer. Get involved. Be a responsible consumer. Take action. And set an example.

Most young people want to help but they don't know how. Often they need mentors, advisors—someone to give them a friendly nudge. If your daughter is always getting caught writing notes to her friends at school, encourage her to use her skills to pen a letter to the president or prime minister about a social issue she cares about. Always on the phone? Suggest volunteering with a help-line. Obsessed with basketball? Why not propose organizing a charity basketball tournament? Always doodling on the table and walls? Why not recommend the creation of a mural for a social or environmental issue? Help young people to seek out their natural skills and talents, nurture them, and open up doors to use them to create a better world. Not everyone's going to fit into the mold of a public speaker, fundraiser, or born leader. That's fine! The movement needs contributions of all kinds. Every person has something valuable to offer!

And to the young people reading these words, don't wait for the adults. Seize the initiative! Choose your issue, do your research, gather a team and take action. Youth are the greatest untapped source of power in the world. When we work together, we are unstoppable!

ADDRESSING ROOT CAUSES

As we've seen, the smallest actions can make a big difference in the lives of the people you meet. Each of these actions is crucial to building a better world. Yet, as you reach out to others and volunteer, you may begin to ask yourself questions about issues. You will wonder, "Why does a particular problem exist?" and seek the underlying structural causes behind it. Maybe there would be less litter in the park if people generated less garbage or if it was possible to return some of the packaging for refunds as we do in the case of beer bottles. Maybe there would be fewer smog warnings if more of us took public transit. Maybe there would be no need to sponsor that child overseas if her family was not forced to sell their crops at a low price because of unfair trade agreements or our desire to buy imports as cheaply as possible.

Last year, a large Free the Children youth group near San Francisco, California, organized a Halloween for Hunger campaign whereby young people went trick-or-treating on Halloween for canned food donations instead of candy.[8] The event was a great success, and the food bank employee gratefully accepted the thousands of pounds of donated goods. He stated that the facility was experiencing a sudden demand in requests because a government housing subsidy had been recently cut, forcing thousands of low-income earners to pay more for their rent. He encouraged the youth involved to continue collecting food goods, but he also challenged them to think about the situation of people living below the poverty line having to choose between paying the increased cost for housing and buying food. The young people from Free the Children decided to learn more about the situation. They ended up organizing a petition and visiting their local government officials to pressure them to reverse the political decision.

Sometimes we come to recognize that if we only address the symptoms of certain social issues, no matter how hard we work, the root causes remain intact.

The struggle between *Me and We* strikes at the heart of much that ails society. Poverty, hunger, homelessness, the destruction of our environment, corporate scandals, government misconduct—all of these issues are simply different names for the same problem: when *Me* steps on *We*.

Some may consider this an oversimplification. But every society, corporation, government, family, and faith group is made up of a collection of people, each of whom faces the daily challenge of balancing "self" and "other." A citizen casts a ballot and chooses the party that best serves him or her, and not the entire country. Someone in a corporation doesn't want to risk losing a pension by blowing the whistle over cancer-causing agents in products. A government official seeks re-election by pandering to special interest groups. These building blocks of choices lead to issues such as insufficient funding for public education, high rates of child leukemia, and a political system awash with "soft money." The most complex issues often break down to the basic question: *Me or We?*

How do we protect the rights of seniors? Keep the city beautiful? Help suffering children? Protect the rainforest? End world poverty? Safeguard the rights of workers? We need to change attitudes. Said plainly, our world would be a better place if all of us thought a little more in the mindset of *We*.

You may find that the basic problem lies in government policies or corporate business practices. In both cases, you have two fundamental tools: a vote and a voice. Throughout history, millions have died in revolutions, wars, and civil rights struggles for democracy. Today, millions more are affected by issues rooted in political choices—people living in poverty, facing discrimination, and struggling without a voice. One of the easiest and most powerful tools to influence systemic change and address root causes is our democratic right and responsibility to vote. As Edmund Burke once said, "All that is required for evil to triumph is for good men to do nothing."

"Democracy is an ongoing process of participation and input into how our society is run effectively and justly. Participate. Stand up. Write letters and sign petitions. Let your elected representatives know who you are and what you think! Similarly, we vote for the business practices and ethics of the corporations we support with each dollar that we spend. It's like our wallets are ballot boxes right next to our bums!"[9]

Marian Wright Edelman once remarked that becoming socially active may simply be "the rent we pay for living."[10] Charity without social action is like using a cup to empty a flooded tub without turning off the tap. Neither will solve the problem in isolation: both are essential to realizing true change in our communities and our world. The key is to mix charity (short-term change through volunteering) with solidarity (long-term change through advocacy).

TAKING THE RISK AND SENDING FORTH THE RIPPLE

We are all interconnected. For people of Faith, this means that we are all God's children. For others, this means that we share a common humanity—something so basic that it ties together all people, regardless of culture, nationality or place of birth.

Me to We embraces the reality that more unites us than divides us—that together we are stronger and can create a better world for ourselves and for future generations.

No matter how you choose to reach out to others to create a more caring society—whether it is through everyday actions at home, working together as a community, engaging your place of worship, or empowering young people—you will be making a critical contribution to the movement from *Me to We*.

As you realize how easy it is and how good it feels to share your gifts and talents, your actions will strengthen your own resolve as an ambassador for this movement. Each time you think in the mindset of *We* and choose to act accordingly, you will inspire others to follow your example. All it takes is one person to stand up, act as a catalyst, and light the spark to inspire others who agree that change is needed, but who are hesitant to come forward to start the chain of events themselves. Once the first person acts, the rest are often embolden to follow.

Let us remember the passion of Robert Kennedy, who said: "Each time a person stands for an ideal, or acts to improve the lot of others, or strikes out against injustice, he or she sends forth a tiny ripple of hope. And crossing each other from a million different centers of energy and daring, those ripples build a current that can sweep down the mightiest walls of oppression and resistance."

My Story

JOE OPATOWSKI

I sometimes think about the person I used to be, and the life I lived. My family was a disaster zone and I counted down the days before I could escape. I recognized most of the police officers who patrolled my neighborhood—they had all taken turns visiting my house on numerous occasions. Fights, and the screaming and yelling that accompanied them, were a matter of routine in my home. My parents would repeatedly get "separated" in a game that often left my brothers and me alone and unsure of what would happen next.

It was even too much for my mom, a woman who had sacrificed almost everything she had—even her sanity—to make ends meet. She did her best to improve our family. We held dinners and tried to talk about our problems. But mostly shouting matches would emerge. Every day things only got worse. Twice my mom disappeared, and I was convinced I would never see her again.

My brother Bobby did manage to escape, if you could call it that. Social workers took him away and placed him in a group home. The day I found out that some of the other boys had pissed on his bed on his first night there I was outraged. When he ran away to the streets and became homeless, I knew it was a decision that I too would have made. Not too long after he chose the streets, someone shoved a lit cigarette up his nose and stole his last $5. I began to lose confidence and faith in the decency of people.

I left home at 17 on a spur-of-the-moment decision with nowhere to go. It was an act of desperation, but one I could not take back. Fortunately, after I'd resigned myself to nights in coffee shops, a friend took me in until I found a landlord who would rent to me even though I was underage. I took multiple jobs to support myself. Market research and telemarketing in the afternoons, waiting tables and deejaying at nights, and even dealing drugs to make spending money. I was still going to high school and trying to balance it all. One teacher kept telling me to stop blaming my problems on my home environment and take control of my life. They just didn't understand.

One day, I met a kid named Jordan, a brilliant and funny person who came from a messed-up home like mine. Jordan told me about a camp that would "change my life." My eyes started to glaze over. *Yeah, right,* I thought. *I don't think so.* I started to turn away. "Did I tell you about the girls?" Jordan added. "There will be a ton of girls. They come from all over the world..." That's all I needed. Where do I sign up?

As I got to know the other youths at this camp, I noticed something different about them. They really *cared*. Not just about the social issues they were fighting for, but about everybody. And they offered me something that I thought only came with big money or a big knife: respect.

I had a great time at the camp and decided to stay involved with this group of new friends. Slowly I started to get involved in their campaigns. Within a year I made a decision that the drug dealing had to go. I realized that I would have to clean up my act, and say goodbye to many other things that had helped me survive in the past. I had to live to a higher standard.

Soon after I made this decision, I was fortunate enough to be sponsored to go with a group of young people to volunteer in the slums of Jamaica.

Riverton, Jamaica. I'm bouncing down a country road in a bus with a group of volunteers, ready to "get involved." I stared out the windows. On either side of the bus were piles and piles of garbage. Suddenly one of the piles moved. A flap opened and out climbed a young boy and an old man. The flap of garbage was the front door to their home. Everyone on the bus went quiet. I felt my face; it was wet with tears.

Climbing out of the bus, we were surrounded by kids, all smiles and expectation. What could I do? I did the only thing I could think of: piggyback rides. I could not get over how unreal the situation was. Here I was in the middle of a garbage dump with some of the poorest kids on earth. We were smiling. We were laughing. It felt good.

Out of breath and seriously thirsty, I wandered over to a street vendor and bought a carton of juice. As I raised it to my mouth, I noticed a small boy with big shining eyes staring up at me. What was I thinking? Guilt quickly kept me from drinking the juice. I handed him the carton. "Here you go, kid, you can have it."

I expected a look of gratitude, but instead I watched the child's face turn serious. I watched him take a deep breath and then walk toward the other children, carton in hand. I couldn't believe my own eyes as I saw this incredibly cute, and incredibly poor little boy making sure that each of his friends had an equal sip. By the time he had finally shared the juice with everyone, he walked over and offered me the carton before he took a sip of his own. To this day, I am left with the fact that I, a kid from North America, took a sip of that juice before a six-year-old kid who lived in a garbage dump.

I quickly realized that it wasn't all about me, after all. I wasn't the only victim. As bad as I had it, somebody always had it worse. And in this case, that somebody—a poverty-stricken little boy—wasn't just surviving. He was *aliving*. This was a lesson I would never forget.

When I got home I decided to make some changes. I brought my family together and told them that I would be there for them—to help see us through the hard times. I shared many of the stories from Jamaica and my past life with anyone who would listen. I spoke to my friends, to youth groups, and even to schools. Soon I was offered a full-time job with the youth organization that had helped me. I am now a member of their speaking bureau and travel across North America to speak to other young people about issues that concern them—youth violence, poverty, cultural diversity, and service to others. I didn't realize how much impact my new life could have until the day I received a phone call at four in the morning. The person on the other end of the line was crying. "I needed someone to talk to. I know you care about me," he said. "That's why I'm still alive." I listened through his sobs as he told me that he had just been standing on the sidewalk, watching an approaching bus, planning on jumping in front of it and ending it all. At the last minute, he'd stepped away and called me instead. My little brother Bobby told me that thanks to me, he would make it through yet another night.

Joe succeded in bringing together his family. He shared his story in speeches to more than 100,000 students across North America. Since the first printing of this book, tragically, Joe lost his life in a car accident on October 29, 2004. His brothers have committed to continuing his work.

Chapter 12:

WRITING YOUR OWN STORY

*"How wonderful it is that nobody need wait a
single moment before starting to improve the world."*
— Anne Frank —
(1929–1945)
Holocaust Victim

For one defining reason, your contribution to the movement
from *Me to We* is critical: You *can* help. If you bought this book
in the self-help aisle, you are more fortunate than the three billion people in the world who live on less than $3 a day. If you
have an acquaintance who lent you this book, then you are
more blessed than the millions of people who, rightly or wrong-
ly, feel that they have no family or friends in the world. Even if
you are sitting in a coffee shop, dental office, library, or school
reading this book, you are still ahead of 80 percent of the
world's population who are illiterate.[1] Some of those people
may live down your street. Some of them may be homeless living "on" your street. They need your help. Help them.

When you finish reading this book, you have a choice. You
can place it back on the shelf and go about your regular life,
pretending that you never saw it (the book also makes a great
doorstop or paperweight); or you can make a promise to yourself, this very moment, that you will start living the *Me to We*
philosophy, contributing to a better world and, therefore, a better you. The actions that you take to make a difference do not

have to be huge. You don't have to travel halfway around the world or start an organization. You can take easy, meaningful actions that change the world in little ways each day, and you can start with your friends, family, co-workers, and neighbors.

Your opportunities to participate in the movement from *Me to We* begin the moment you wake up. So many simple, easy gestures can change the world—one person at a time. The sum of these gestures over the course of a day, a week, a year, and a lifetime—practiced by one, and then two, and then a dozen, and then a million people—can create enormous positive change. We can start by being more conscious and caring of individuals in our immediate lives and then become more aware of ways in which we can embrace people in the wider community.

ISSUE + GIFT = BETTER WORLD (...AND BETTER YOU!)

Throughout this book, you have read the stories of people who live the *Me to We* philosophy. You have been introduced to individuals like Lindsay Avner, who is taking action to save her own life, that of her mother, and millions of others whom she has never met, by participating in the race to find a cure for breast cancer; the renowned Jane Goodall, who lovingly describes the chimpanzees she lived with for decades, and who has been working tirelessly to educate people, especially young people, about protecting our natural environment; and John Gaither, who is spending his senior years volunteering and helping to inspire the next generation of civically minded youth.

We hope that in reading about these heroes, you have found their courage and inner beauty inspiring. However, the greatest tribute you can provide to them is not a tear or a smile, but to translate your inspiration into action. The broader purpose of these profiles is to inform you about some of the most important challenges we face as individuals and as the human race. At the end of this book, you will find concrete actions you can take to help address the social issues brought to light by each of these stories. You will also be provided with facts and statistics that reveal the scope of these problems, to which you can lend your time, energy, passion, and expertise. All this information can help you to *write your own story*: to draw inspiration from these pages and act now to create a better society and a better you.

If the examples presented here have not resonated with you, or if you don't have a vision for your action just yet, don't worry! Simply by having read these stories, you have become more attuned to the pressing problems and challenges facing the people of the world and will soon find an issue that moves you. And don't be overwhelmed—keep in mind that few of the people featured here are celebrities, and none are professional world-changers. They are for the most part everyday people like you with one basic element in common: they saw a need, they had something to give, and they gave it. It's often that simple.

Once you have found your issue, the next step is to match it with your gift and then start writing your own story! This is the equation for a better world. We all have skills and talents, but so often we don't realize that they are gifts that we can share with the world. Craig learned this lesson a few years ago, while he was doing a television interview on a show that was focusing on "accomplished youth." The other young interviewee was 19 years old, had already completed his Masters degree and PhD, and was working at an important job at a pharmaceutical company. He kept mentioning that he was "gifted," a fact that he had discovered in grade three, when he passed a special IQ test where one circles a number of boxes on sheets of paper, which are then run through a computer to determine how gifted or average one is. The boy's parents told him that he was "gifted"; his teachers spent extra time with him because he was "gifted" and the media labelled him as "gifted." He must have said the word "gifted" at least five times during the interview. Finally, the host turned to Craig and asked, "Well ... are you gifted, Craig?" Craig looked at her and shook his head, "No."

Later that day, Craig was still thinking about the interview when he went back to the Free the Children office. As he looked around at the remarkable young people who work with us, he realized that he had given the host the wrong answer. Craig saw our web master—whom we all consider to be incredibly gifted when it comes to designing websites that are visited by millions of people around the world. He saw our young writing staff, who are talented at translating their passion and energy into words that inspire others. He saw our amazing adult volunteers, who are gifted mentors, and who give tirelessly of their time and expertise. Craig thought of all the people who are talented with their hands, compassionate listeners, great at raising money or brilliant in art or music. He thought of people who build our homes and take care of our sick, who teach in our schools, and who recycle our garbage to protect the environment. In fact, he could not think of anyone he knew who wasn't gifted. Craig realized that each one of us is born with talents. We are all gifted in some way, but not in every way. We are naturally interdependent. We all need one another. Like pieces of a puzzle, each one of us has important things to contribute in our place and time, to create a mosaic of a good and caring society where all people can grow and develop to their fullest potential. Only by sharing our gifts can we achieve a better world.

Think about what you love to do, or what interests you. Whether its sports, or art, or working with children—what lights you up is often where you'll find your gifts. If your gifts are empathy and listening, you can be known around your school or place of work as someone whom people can always talk to, or you can volunteer at a support center for drug addicts, abused women, or street youth. If your gift is business or accounting related, you can help low-income families with their tax returns, or volunteer to help a local charity improve its infrastructure and efficiency or prepare for an audit. If your gift is research, you can help develop a social justice campaign on an issue that you feel passionate about. If your gift is sports or arts related, you can donate your time and talent to a local charity for a fundraising event, concert, or exhibition. If you are caring, brave, friendly, perceptive, organized, funny, patient, motivated, likeable, handy, trustworthy, calming, disciplined, sensitive, or anything else, you can help in your own way. *Everyone has a gift to contribute!*

As you begin your journey, you may question whether you have truly found "your issue" or whether "your gift" will make a difference. You may face self-doubt and wonder if you have made the right choice or are really prepared to take the first step—but don't worry; no one has all the answers. We learned this lesson from a great teacher. We were in Stockholm at an international conference, where 30 of the most eminent minds of our time, including the Dalai Lama, had come together to discuss a number of critical social issues. At one point, someone stood up and asked him a long, elaborate, highly complex question. It took this individual about six minutes to ask his question. The Dalai Lama, however, listened carefully, took some notes, and after a long moment looked up and responded:

"I don't know."

There was a moment of silence. Then, glancing around the room, we noticed a little smile on nearly everyone's face. We had all expected the Dalai Lama to come up with some pearl of wisdom that would enlighten us all. Instead, with three words, he dispelled the myth that one must be all-knowing and all-powerful in order to influence the world. This great leader taught us a powerful lesson that day–that there is no magic answer. There are only people, a growing multitude of people, reaching out to help others with dedication, passion, and sincerity. And there is magic in that.

SCARCITY OR ABUNDANCE

Sometimes it's easy for all of us to forget just how much we have to give, and to throw out the same old excuses for not acting:

"I'm just scraping by myself."

"I don't have the time."

"Others are better off, but they're not helping ... so why should I?"

"There is only so much to go around" is the greatest fallacy of our time. How can we tell someone dying in the hospital that we don't have enough time to give blood? How can we tell the person sleeping on the street that the dozen-plus outfits in our closets are barely enough for our needs?

Instead of focusing on what we feel is lacking or *scarce,* why not celebrate what we do have in *abundance*–operating on the principle that there is always enough to go around?[2] Every one of us has an abundance of time, energy, and compassion, if we choose to make a priority of sharing it with others.

Think of the people who have made some of the greatest contributions to a better world: Mahatma Gandhi. Nelson Mandela. Terry Fox. Rick Hansen. Mother Teresa. What did they have that we don't (besides centuries of colonial oppression, a 30-year prison term, cancer, paralysis from the waist down, and multitudes of poor people at their doorstep)?

The decision to help others is not related to our ability to do so, but to our choices and priorities. In sharing our gifts, what we feel is not a sense of loss or depletion, but often a great discovery of abundance. Living the *Me to We* philosophy has a strange way of making us all realize just how much we have to offer—and this knowledge can give each and every one of us a greater positive self-image, a *real* feeling of purpose, and a deeper appreciation of life itself.

Of the many lessons that we have learned throughout our travels, none has been more valuable and lasting than this principle of abundance. We remember the little boy in Thailand who, given a precious orange, breaks it apart and shares it with his friends, the street children who have no parents but maintain the courage to survive, or the countless thousands of pre-teen and teenaged girls around the globe who raise their siblings on their own after being orphaned by AIDS, hunger, or war.

Our work with Free the Children took Craig to Salvador on the coast of Brazil where he spent time with street and working children. With the help of a translator, he started talking with a boy, about 14 years old, who was shining shoes on the side of the street. After Craig gained his trust, the boy brought him to his home, a bus shelter that he shared with his friends. At night, they would cover themselves with cardboard and newspapers to stay warm. As Craig entered the simple structure, the children were very careful to make sure that no police were around.

In Brazil and many other South American countries, street children are often seen as petty criminals, vermin, and drug pushers. Members of the police are frequently hired by business people to remove them from the streets in front of their shops. Many of these children "disappear." Some are tossed into jail without any charges or placed in cells with adults who abuse them harshly. Others are driven to rural areas and dumped, or simply killed.

As Craig sat among the children in the bus shelter, they each told him the story of how they had ended up on the streets. Some had been sent away from home because the rain didn't fall, the crops didn't grow, and there was simply not enough food for the whole family—it was up to the oldest child to find work in the city. Others had run away from homes where they were being physically or sexually abused by their parents, relatives, or people in the community. Finding themselves alone in the city streets, they turned to each other to survive: ranging in age from eight to 16 years old, these children came together as a family. They looked to each other for a sense of security, sharing the food and money they had gathered, watching out for each other, coming to each other's aid. They had little in the way of material possessions, but they did have one another. There was a sense of belonging and unity among them that was unbreakable.

At one point during Craig's visit, the kids asked him if he wanted to play a game of soccer with them, and he agreed. Suddenly, one of the boys dashed off around the corner. He returned a minute later, holding a plastic water bottle he had found among the garbage on the street. He let it drop to the ground and started kicking it around: they had a ball! Most of the children had two possessions—a pair of shorts and a T-shirt. They did not own shoes—they were all barefoot. Not one among them would have owned a soccer ball, but that didn't keep them from the game. They played for hours that day, until finally, in one of the scuffles, someone fell on the bottle and crushed it. They all sank down on the side of the street, exhausted and totally content.

Craig had to leave the next day, and as he said goodbye to his new friends, the leader of the group, a 14-year-old boy named José, came forward. He wanted to give Craig a gift by which to remember the street kids. He stood there for a moment, looking down at his hands, thinking. Suddenly, he broke into a smile. He took off his T-shirt, a red and white soccer jersey of his favorite team, folded it carefully, and handed it to Craig.

Craig was dumbfounded. José stood there shirtless, not expecting anything in return. To him, Craig had already given them all a precious gift. Most people just ignore the street kids, spit on them, beat them up. Instead, Craig had shown them respect. Craig was an outsider, of a different color and nationality, yet these street children embraced him as one of their friends, a member of their community. Craig said that he couldn't accept the shirt, but José insisted, proud to have something to offer. So Craig took off his simple white T-shirt, folded it, and handed it to his new friend in return.

Craig still has that soccer jersey. When he came home, he framed it and hung it on his wall in his bedroom to remind him of the lesson the street children had taught him: if everyone had the heart of a 14-year-old street child, there would be no more poverty, injustice, or suffering in the world.

We don't have all the answers, but embracing a *Me to We* philosophy has changed our lives. When we first started becoming socially involved a decade ago, we never expected that it would take us from the suburbs of North America to the slums and war zones of the world. We never dreamed that it would lead to improving the lives of millions of children or sharing our stories with you. We never thought that it would provide us with true happiness and friendships and fulfillment. But it has. In reaching out to others, all of this came to be. We have written this book because we have seen what is possible.

In Peace,
Craig and Marc

My Story

ANONYMOUS

We would like to conclude with a final story. This is the story of an individual with remarkable skills and talents. This person has vision, energy, and passion. This person has the power to change the world by reaching out to others—but was awaiting a call. One day, the call came. It didn't take much—there was no epiphany, no cloud opening. All it took was a gentle push.

With a little inspiration, this individual will go on to do great things, contributing to a better world in a unique and personal way. Although these remarkable actions won't make front-page news, they will be permanent etchings in the sands of time, forever remembered by the people who will be touched by them.

The positive energy, born of this one person, will spread like a ripple inspiring others to join a powerful movement to help others. This individual will embody the Movement from *Me to We* and make his or her life more meaningful, fulfilling, and happier than he or she ever dreamt possible.

Who is this person? We hope it will be you.

We don't know how this story will end, but we know how it can continue—with a simple gesture—one first act of giving that will set off a chain of events. We hope that you will gently push another person along this same journey, by now passing this book to someone special in your life.

Stories, Facts, and Actions

KIM PHUC
ISSUE:

Peace and War-Affected Children

FACTS:

- Over two million children have died and more than six million children have been injured by war in the past decade.
- There are currently more than 10 million child refugees.
- More than 31,000 nuclear weapons are still maintained by the eight known nuclear powers.

ACTIONS:

- Encourage the children in your life to play with non-violent games and toys.
- Fundraise to build a school in a post-conflict region through *Free the Children*.
- Write a letter to your political representatives promoting peacekeeping and diplomatic efforts to avert war.

KEITH TAYLOR
ISSUE:

Poverty

FACTS:

- Studies by the Institute for Policy Studies and United for a Fair Economy reveal that "29% of working families do not earn a living wage, and of these families, 70% experience real hardships—having to skip meals or rent payments or forgo needed medical care."
- By 2002, the CEO-worker pay gap stood at 282:1, almost seven times the 1982 ratio of 42:1. The wealth of the world's

225 richest individuals is equal to the annual income of the poorest 47 percent, or 2.5 billion people.

- The 2002 World Summit on Sustainable Development reported that 15 percent of the world's population living in high-income countries consume 56 percent of the Earth's resources, while the poorest 40 percent, in low-income countries, consume only 11 percent of its resources.

ACTIONS:

- Gather a group of friends to bring food, warm clothes, and friendship to the homeless in your city, or order some extra food when dining out and take it "to go" to give to someone who asks you for change on the street.
- Make an effort to live more simply. Look around your home for excess clothing or household items that you rarely use and donate them to a service organization. Organize a dress-down day at your school or workplace to raise funds for a worthy cause.
- Make the decision to set aside a certain amount of money every week or month to donate to your favorite charity.

TIM LEFENS

ISSUE:

Engaging People with Disabilities

FACTS:

- Approximately 15 percent of North Americans suffer from a disability.
- Over 16 million non-institutionalized North Americans have a severe physical disability that prevents them from performing regular functions.
- Approximately 10 million of non-institutionalized North Americans need personal assistance daily.

ACTIONS:
- Give a break for a few hours to a parent who has a child with a physical or mental disability. Contact a home for people with disabilities and enquire about volunteer opportunities.
- Employers: Hire people with disabilities and become an equal opportunity employer and encourage others to do the same. Make your workplace wheelchair accessible.
- Participate in a March of Dimes walk, help with the Special Olympics, or read to the blind. Take a disabled person to the park. Support people with disabilities in their efforts to live a full life and encourage others to do the same.

JONATHAN WHITE
ISSUE:

Reaching out and Connecting with People

FACTS:
- In a national survey of older Americans in 2003, 46 percent said that they are very or somewhat worried about "being lonely and feeling isolated."
- In the United States, half the women over the age of 75 live alone.
- In Canada, the proportion of one-person households had risen from about one-fifth of all households in 1981 to more than one in four by 2001.

ACTIONS:
- Call your wife or husband, mother or father, or grandmother or grandfather and tell them that you love them.
- Visit an elderly person who is living alone and offer your friendship and help with errands.
- Help a new person, especially an immigrant, in your school or workplace make friends and feel welcome. Volunteer for an organization that integrates new immigrants into the community.

ARCHBISHOP DESMOND TUTU

ISSUE:

Working against Discrimination

FACTS:

- There are 250 million people in the world today who suffer under some form of apartheid, modern-day slavery, or other extreme forms of discrimination because they were born into a marginalized class.
- Since the 1960s the number of immigrants to Canada from Europe and the United States has decreased while the presence of immigrants of visible minorities has risen. Visible minorities represent 80 percent of immigrants in the period 1991 to 1996.
- *USA Today* reported that in a 2004 Gallup Poll, 76 percent of caucasians in the United States, including nine of ten under 30, thought African-Americans are now being treated very fairly or somewhat fairly. By contrast, only 38 percent of African-Americans agreed.

ACTIONS:

- Speak up when you hear someone use a racist slur or tell a racist joke.
- Organize or patronize a multicultural celebration in your community.
- Join a local or national organization that fights against discrimination and works to protect and uphold the rights of all people.

RICHARD GERE

ISSUE:

Putting Faith and Spirituality into Action

FACTS:

- In the past three to four decades, North Americans have become about 10 percent less likely to claim membership in various religious denominations, while actual attendance and involvement in religious activities has fallen approximately 50 percent.

- In a 2003 CNN / USA Today poll, 92 percent of Americans surveyed say that they believe in the existence of God and 51 percent believe that religion is losing its influence on American life.
- American religious communities spend roughly $15 billion to $20 billion annually on social service programs.

ACTIONS:

- Translate your faith into action through service to others.
- Learn about other people's understandings of spirituality and faith.
- Take part in or help to form an interfaith coalition regarding pressing issues (community needs, youth violence, AIDS, debt of poor countries ...).

DR. JANE GOODALL

ISSUE:

Environmental Protection

FACTS:

- During the 1990s, the estimated combined loss of the world's forests was 94 million hectares—an area larger than Venezuela.
- By 2015, half of the total annual destruction of the ozone layer will be the result of air travel.
- Excessive use of fertilizers is disrupting coastal ecosystems and adding to the depletion of fish stocks.

ACTIONS:

- Create "garbage-free" days at your school or place of work; use public transportation; organize a community clean-up day; plant trees.
- If you are a young person, start a Roots and Shoots club. Visit www.janegoodall.org for more information.

- Make your voice heard! Let politicians know that you care about important conservation issues by writing letters, sending e-mails, and signing petitions.

OPRAH WINFREY
ISSUE:

Reaching out to the Global Community

FACTS:
- Between 57 percent and 75 percent of children in South Africa are living in poverty of varying degrees.
- In 2004, there were 5 million people living with HIV/AIDS, and 660,000 children orphaned by AIDS in South Africa. The country's aggregate under-five mortality rate is 59 per 1,000 live births, but the rate for Africans (63) is four times higher than that of whites (15).
- In South Africa, there is a high school enrolment rate of over 80 percent, but there are high repetition rates at all levels, high dropout rates, and an adult illiteracy rate of 33 percent.

ACTIONS:
- Educate yourself on the social and political issues facing South African society, and spread the word about what you've learned. Participate in a petition campaign to have your government increase its contribution to the Global Fund to Fight AIDS, Tuberculosis and Malaria.
- Think about the issues of child poverty, HIV/AIDS, and the state of education in your own community. Lend your support to a local organization working to address one or more of these problems.
- Contribute to the mission to support, educate, and uplift AIDS-affected children by donating to Oprah's Angel Network

through Network for Good. Follow the online format or send donations payable to Oprah's Angel Network to:

Oprah's Angel Network

P.O. Box 96600

Chicago, IL 60693

KATHY BUCKLEY

ISSUE:

Depression and Suicide

FACTS:

- The World Health Organization reports that five of the ten leading causes of disability are related to mental health disorders.
- Depression is a common illness that each year affects 18.8 million American adults (nearly one in ten). Depression does not discriminate; it affects men and women, young and old, and people of all races, cultures, and incomes.
- There are approximately 31,000 suicides every year in the United States; suicides in the United States outnumber homicides by a margin of three to two.

ACTIONS:

- Smile. Lend a friendly ear to someone who is having a bad day. Be conscious of the moods and emotions of people in your life. Be aware of the signs of loneliness, depression, and suicide.
- Increase awareness of mental health problems by researching the topic and informing others, especially during Mental Heath Week.
- Volunteer at a crisis counseling organization, such as Kids Help Phone or a drop-in center for the homeless suffering from a mental illness. Visit a mental health institution to help brighten the day for patients.

JOHN GAITHER
ISSUE:

Engaging a Lifetime of Experience

FACTS:

- Only 14 percent of people 65 and over were in the U.S. labor force in the year 2000. One in three North Americans over the age of 65 says that they do not have enough social activity in their lives.
- In 20 years, the population of persons 65 and over in the United States will double as baby boomers retire. In 2050, there will be more than 80 million Americans over the age of 65.
- According to the Fraser Institute, in the next 50 years, the proportion of the population aged 65 and over in Canada will double.

ACTIONS:

- Take part in a grandparent/grandchild volunteer activity. Research your family tree, involving all generations.
- When voting, buying goods, or allocating your retirement time, ask what type of legacy you want to leave your children and grandchildren.
- Leave a legacy or bequest in your will to build a school in your name or in the name of a loved one.

JORDANA WEISS
ISSUE:

Education

FACTS:

- Around the world, 130 million children (two-thirds of them girls) are denied the chance to go to school. Another 150 million children drop out of primary school before they have completed five years of education; 862 million people, or one in four adults in the developing world, cannot read or write.

- In North America, 22 percent of adults have low-level literacy skills. They have difficulty dealing with printed material and understanding reading instructions.
- "Education is a human right with immense power to transform. On its foundation rest the cornerstones of freedom, democracy and sustainable human development."–Kofi Annan, Secretary General of the United Nations

ACTIONS:
- Read to your children. Go to the library. Collect books from garage sales. Develop in your children a love of reading.
- Volunteer as a reading mentor at your neighborhood school, local community center, library, immigrant drop-in center, or boys' and girls' club.
- Fundraise to pay for a teacher's salary or to build a classroom or school in the developing world.

LINDSAY AVNER

ISSUE:

Breast Cancer

FACTS:
- In the United Sates, one woman is diagnosed with breast cancer every three minutes, and one woman will die of breast cancer every 12 minutes.
- In Canada, one in nine women is expected to develop breast cancer during her lifetime. One in 27 will die of it.
- Early detection through screening is our best defense against morbidity and mortality from breast and cervical cancers and pre-cancers.

ACTIONS:
- Encourage the women in your life to exercise responsible breast health through monthly breast self-examinations, clinical breast exams, and screening mammography.

- Donate or fundraise to help find a cure for breast cancer and proudly wear the pink ribbon, drawing awareness to the cause.
- Help in the organization of your local Race for the Cure or similar breast cancer runs and recruit fellow runners to participate.

JOE OPATOWSKI

ISSUE:

Engaging Youth to Be Social Changemakers

FACTS:

- There are approximately 90 million young people between the ages of five and 24 in North America.
- More than the half of the teens in a 2001 national U.S. survey expressed their desire for more community after-school programs, and two-thirds said they would participate in such initiatives if they were available.
- Young people in Canada reflect less of a sense of civic process than older citizens. For example, in an Elections Canada Study (2000), in response to the statement "If I did not vote, I would feel guilty," only 18 percent of respondents in the youngest age category expressed agreement, compared to 34 percent in the oldest category.

ACTIONS:

- Spend time with your teenage daughter or son. Do fun things together. Schedule a time to volunteer side by side.
- Bring your children with you when you vote to expose them to the electoral process. Visit your city or town hall; sit in on a session of your local government council; introduce your children to their local politicians. Encourage young people to contact politicians regarding issues that concern them.
- If you are a young person, consider starting a Free the Children chapter in your school.

About the Contributors

LINDSAY AVNER

Lindsay Avner has worked with the Susan G. Komen Breast Cancer Foundation for five years and has become a well-known national advocate in involving young people in the fight against breast cancer. She currently consults, trains, and mentors Komen Leadership and student leaders across the United States. Her dream is to see the end of breast cancer. More information on Lindsay's work can be found at www.komen.org.

KATHY BUCKLEY

Actress, comedienne, author, and motivational speaker, Kathy Buckley delivers the message that anything can be achieved when the heart and mind work together. She embodies her mission in life, namely, "I love to make people laugh, but I love it even more if I can teach them something at the same time." For more information on Kathy Buckley, visit www.kathybuckley.com.

DR. JOHN GAITHER

Dr. John Gaither is a retired educator who lives in Toronto, Ontario, with his wife, Dorothea, a clinical psychologist in private practice. Since his retirement in 1999 as a high school principal, he has been an enthusiastic volunteer with Free the Children and serves as its School Building Projects Coordinator. He has traveled on a number of occasions with youths to the developing world. He is young at heart and highly respected for his work with young people.

RICHARD GERE

Richard Gere is a well-known actor, humanitarian, and philanthropist. Success on stage and in film have allowed him the stature and means to focus attention on the Chinese occupation of Tibet. For more than 20 years, Gere has been inspired by His Holiness the Dalai Lama to help relieve suffering around the world. Through his foundation, Gere supports survivors of war and natural disasters, world health relief, and basic human rights. More information on his work is available at www.gerefoundation.org.

DR. JANE GOODALL

Dr. Jane Goodall met the anthropologist Dr. Louis Leakey in 1957 and soon afterwards began to work for him in Africa. Her research, based on extensive field work, is considered a milestone in the study of primatology. Goodall is the author of numerous books, including *In the Shadow of Man* and *My Life with the Chimpanzees*. In 1995 she was presented the CBE by Queen Elizabeth. She founded the Jane Goodall Institute in 1977. More information on her work and that of her youth outreach program, Roots and Shoots, is available at www.janegoodall.org.

TIM LEFENS

Tim Lefens, founder and executive director of A.R.T. (Artistic Realization Technologies), lives in Belle Mead, New Jersey. He is author of the book *Flying Colors*, a moving account of overcoming limitations and the power of creative expression. Tim is the recipient of the Pollock-Krasner Award for Painting and the Robert Wood Johnson Foundation Community Health Leadership Award. He continues to work to share A.R.T.'s significant breakthroughs through training sessions, lecture seminars, and book readings. More information on Tim's work can be found at www.artrealization.org.

JOE OPATOWSKI

Joe Opatowski was an extraordinary member of the Free The Children team. He traveled extensively in the developing world, accompanying young people on volunteer trips to Ecuador, Jamaica and Mexico. He facilitated leadership programs for the Young Presidents' Organization (YPO), the Institute for Civic Leadership, and numerous youth conferences and gatherings. He addressed over 100,000 students across North America, spreading a message of empowerment and service to others. On October 29, 2004, Joe tragically lost his life in a car accident. He just 21 years old.

Joe's life was his message. He continues to inspire us. A scholarship fund has been established in his memory to allow young people the same opportunity to transform their lives through volunteering overseas. For more information, contact info@freethechildren.com.

KIM PHUC

Kim Phuc became world famous when she was photographed as a young girl running naked down a highway, her skin on fire from napalm. Her picture became the defining image of the Vietnam War. Kim Phuc now runs the Kim Foundation, a non-profit organization committed to funding programs to heal children in war-torn areas of the world. Kim is also a UNESCO Goodwill Ambassador. More information on Kim's work is available at www.kimfoundation.com.

DEEPA SHANKARAN

Deepa Shankaran is a long-time Free the Children and *Leaders Today* team member who has traveled widely and helped to facilitate volunteer programs in Thailand and in Kenya. She has researched and written human rights-related materials and articles for the *Geneva News and International Report*, the World Health organization, and Free the Children. She co-authored *Take More Action*, a book on civic education for students.

KEITH TAYLOR

Keith Taylor is a professor of medieval literature at Middle Tennessee State University and the founder of Modest Needs, an Internet site that provides small financial assistance to those in need. Combining donations and $400 a month from his own income, he has been able to fulfill his lifelong dream of becoming a philanthropist. More information on Keith's work is available at www.modestneeds.org.

ARCHBISHOP DESMOND TUTU

Desmond Tutu was the first black Anglican archbishop of Cape Town, South Africa. He rose to worldwide fame in the 1980s for his opposition to apartheid. On October 16, 1984, he was awarded the Nobel Peace Prize. During the 1990s, he headed the Truth and Reconciliation Commission in South Africa. He is the author of numerous books, including *No Future without Forgiveness*, and holds honorary doctorate degrees from dozens of leading universities around the world. Desmond Tutu is an honorary member of Free the Children's Board of Directors.

JORDANA WEISS

Jordana Weiss is currently 15 years old and a Grade 10 student in Thornhill, Ontario. She has been actively involved with Free the Children since the age of nine. She is a member of Free the Children's speaking bureau and often addresses students and community organizations. In her spare time, she enjoys Shakespearean plays and learning about different languages and cultures. She is looking forward to traveling to India in the not too distant future.

DR. JONATHAN WHITE

Dr. Jonathan White is professor of sociology and political economy at Colby College in Maine. He is the Founding Director of

Sports for Hunger, the Hunger Resource Center, and Halloween for Hunger. Professor White has authored numerous articles on the issue of inequality in the United States as well as materials relating to globalization. He is currently finishing a book entitled *Hungry to Be Heard: Voices from a Malnourished America*, to be published by Oxford University Press.

OPRAH WINFREY

Oprah Winfrey has already left an indelible mark on the face of television. From her humble beginnings in rural Mississippi, Oprah's legacy has established her as one of the most important figures in popular culture. Her contributions can be felt beyond the world of television and into areas such as publishing, music, film, philanthropy, education, health and fitness, and social awareness. As supervising producer and host of *The Oprah Winfrey Show*, Oprah entertains, enlightens, and empowers millions of viewers around the world.

KIM ZARZOUR

Kim Zarzour is a freelance writer and author whose work has been published in national magazines and featured on radio. She is a former newspaper reporter and author of several books on parenting. Between writing assignments, she tends to her three children, golden retriever Boomer, and her husband in their home near Toronto, Canada.

About the Authors

CRAIG KIELBURGER is the founder and chair of Free the Children, an international children's charity that has improved the lives of over one million young people in 35 countries. Craig's work has been profiled on *Oprah, 60 Minutes,* CNN, and CBC, and in the *New York Times, The Economist, Time,* and *People Magazine.* He was named a Global Leader of Tomorrow by the World Economic Forum and is the recipient of the Franklin D. Roosevelt Freedom Medal and the State of the World Forum Award. Craig is much in demand as a speaker and has traveled to more than 40 countries, speaking out in defense of children's rights. His first book, *Free the Children,* has been translated into eight languages and was the winner of the Christopher Book Award. Craig has since co-authored two more books with his brother, Marc. Craig attends the University of Toronto, where he is pursuing a degree in Peace and Conflict Studies. He has been twice nominated for the Nobel Peace Prize.

MARC KIELBURGER is a Harvard graduate, Rhodes Scholar, and Oxford-educated lawyer. He co-founded Leaders Today in 1998 with his brother, Craig, with the vision of providing leadership training to young people who wish to become involved in social issues. The programs reach over 250,000 young people annually. Leaders Today has provided leadership training to youth for the United Nations, State of the World Forum, and dozens of school boards throughout North America. He co-authored *Take Action!* and *Take More Action*—civics books that are used by thousands of students. His work has been featured on CBC, BBC, and CNN, among many other news and print media. He was recently chosen by Canada's business community as one of the country's "Top 40 leaders under the age of 40."

Free the Children

"Children Helping Children"

Free the Children is a unique international organization of children helping children through education, leadership, and peace-building. The purpose of the organization is not only to free children from poverty and exploitation, but also to free young people from the idea that they are powerless to change the world. Founded in 1995 by Craig Kielburger, Free the Children has since involved more than one million young people around the world in its projects.

Free the Children's main emphasis is on the promotion of education as the solution to many of today's social issues. Recognizing the fact that over 130 million of the world's poorest children do not attend school, two-thirds of whom are girls, Free the Children has raised funds to build 400 schools in 21 developing countries, providing daily education to over 35,000 children. Free the Children also supports income-generating initiatives that empower poor families, enabling children to go to school, and ships school and medical supplies to children in need. These campaigns provide young people with the skills and opportunities they require to take action on behalf of their peers.

Free the Children is comprised of passionate young people and adult supporters of all ages who wish to change the world. There are many ways for you to become involved and make a difference in the lives of children around the globe, including

- Researching important issues such as child poverty, child exploitation, education, and children's rights in North America and on an international level and educating others about what they can do to help.
- Fundraising to provide the gift of education to children in developing countries; send school supplies, pay for a teacher's salary, or help build a classroom.
- Starting a Free the Children group in your school or community.

Please visit www.freethechildren.com for more information on how to become involved.

Free the Children
233 Carlton St., Toronto, Ontario, Canada M5A 2L2
Phone: (416) 925-5894   Fax: (416) 925-8242
USA phone: 1-800-203-9091
info@freethechildren.com   www.freethechildren.com

Leaders Today

"We are the generation that we have been waiting for ..."

Leaders Today believes that leadership development is the key to achieving a generation of committed and socially active young people. Leaders Today was founded by Marc and Craig Kielburger in 1998 and motivates and educates tens of thousands of young people around the world each year.

Leaders Today offers unique opportunities to unlock the leadership potential of all young people, through providing programs in global citizenship, character education, and community service.

- International Volunteer Opportunities: Leaders Today organizes and facilitates global volunteer trips to Kenya, Ecuador, Nicaragua, Mexico, India, and Thailand. Trip highlights include building a primary school, teaching English, leadership programming, language lessons, and life-long friendships.
- International Leadership and Volunteer Centers: Leaders Today has two beautiful leadership and volunteer centers that accept school or religious groups and short- or long-term volunteers throughout the academic year. Located in the Masai Mara region of Kenya and in Patagonia, Arizona (on the U.S./Mexico border), these centers are ideal for volunteerism and leadership opportunities.
- Global Leadership Programs: Leaders Today facilitators can come to your school, conference, or place of worship to teach leadership skills. Leaders Today offers leadership academies during the summer and March Break periods in Toronto, Ontario, and Patagonia, Arizona.
- Motivational Speakers and Speaking Tours: Leaders Today has world-class youth motivational speakers who are ideal for youth gatherings or events.
- School Board Partnerships: Leaders Today works with many of the largest school boards across North America to administer leadership programs and coordinate volunteer initiatives.

Please visit www.leaderstoday.com for more information on how you can gain the skills, confidence, and experiences to change the world.

Leaders Today
233 Carlton St., Toronto, Ontario, Canada M5A 2L2
Phone: (416) 964-8942   Fax: (416) 925-8242
info@leaderstoday.com   www.leaderstoday.com

Acknowledgments

Our gratitude to Deepa Shankaran and Dr. Jonathan White for serving as associate editors of the project. A special thank you to Kim Zarzour for her dedication and patience and to Ed "the fun guy" Gillis for his humor and energy. Thank you to Shelley Page for her words of inspiration; Eva and Yoel Haller for their love; Lekha Singh for her guidance; Virginia Benderly for her wisdom; John Gaither for his thousands of hours spent volunteering and Dr. Dorothea Gaither for her insight; and Roxanne Joyal for her unwavering support over the past eight years.

Our appreciation goes out to the team at John Wiley & Sons Canada, especially Robert Harris and Don Loney for their tremendous support and belief in the project. We were fortunate to have so many gifted and inspiring contributors to the book, including Archbishop Desmond Tutu, Oprah Winfrey, Dr. Jane Goodall, Kim Phuc, Richard Gere, Tim Lefens, Lindsay Avner, Vicky Collins, Kathy Buckley, Jordana Weiss, the Johnstone family, Chris Delaney, Deb Merkely, Joe Opatowski, Keith Taylor, June Callwood, Buddy Winston, and Greg Harmandayan.

Thanks also to Ylva Van Buren, Lynne Ainsworth, Kathleen Ruff, Toinette Bezant, Sheila Dabu, Helen Keeler, Shelley White, Greg Rogers, Robyn Brentano, Janice Shoening, Jocelyn Land-Murphy, Marisa Antonello, Mary Lewis, Bartek Kosinski, Shobha Sharma, Chris Besse, and Jennifer Holland for their assistance, as well as Jocelyn Sweet, Matthew Regan, Danielle Lefebvre, Catherine Connors, Carolyn Reimer, Andrea McKenzie, and Jaime Forsythe for their research.

Our work would not be possible without the help of Free the Children supporters and members of the board of directors, both in Canada and in the United States, and the Free the Children and Leaders Today team, especially all the young people.

Our gratitude to the organizations and individuals who believe in our mission. In this respect, we include Diane Hudson and Katy Davis from Harpo, Caren Yanis from the Angel Network, David Krieger and The Nuclear Age Peace Foundation, Leonard Kurz and The Kurz Family Foundation, Julie Toskan-Casale and the Toskan Foundation, Linda Rosier and the Concept 3 Advertising Team, Pi Media Partners, The i2 Foundation, The Singh Foundation, Buzz Hargrove and the Canadian Auto Workers' Union, Joseph Koch, Vito Maltese, Leo Ciccone, the Apostolopoulos family, the Joyal family, the Weiss family, the Rubin family, and the Heimark family.

Our family deserves a heartfelt thank you, especially our Mimi, who remains our biggest fan. Finally, and most importantly, we would not be where we are without the love and continuous support of our parents, Fred and Theresa. Thank you for everything, Mom and Dad, we love you!

Endnotes

CHAPTER 1:

1. David G. Myers, "Wealth, Well-Being, and the New American Dream," Center for a New American Dream http://www.newdream.org/discuss/myers.html (9 June 2004).

2. Daniel McGinn, "Self Help USA," *Newsweek*, 10 January 2000.

3. "The Road Well Trodden: How to Succeed in Publishing," *The Economist*, 17 May 2001.

4. Ibid.

5. Robyn William, "The Dark Side of the Australian Dream," *Radio National*, 20 June 1999.

6. Belinda S. Ray, *Gale Encyclopedia of Popular Culture*, 26 January 2004.

7. Social critic Wendy Kaminer, the author of *I'm Dysfunctional, You're Dysfunctional*, calls many of the self-help books on the market comprised of "grandly meaningless, vaguely spiritual phrases," largely irrelevant to the life of the reader. For further discussion, see Wendy Kaminer, *I'm Dysfunctional, You're Dysfunctional: The Recovery Movement and Other Self-Help Fashions* (Reading, MA: Addison-Wesley, 1992), p. 106. This sentiment is echoed by psychologist Annie Murphy Paul, who writes that, "often, the messages of self-help books tend to be vast oversimplifications, misrepresenting a part of the truth for the whole." Annie Murphy Paul, "Self-Help: Shattering the Myths," *Psychology Today*, March 2001 http://www.findarticles.com/cf_dls/m1175/2_34/71189922/print.jhtml (26 January 2004).

8. Worldwatch Institute, "State of the World 2004: Consumption by the Numbers," http://www.worldwatch.org/press/news/2004/01/07/ (1 April 2004).

9. David G. Myers, "The American Paradox: Chapter One," excerpted from David G. Myers, *The American Paradox: Spiritual Hunger in an Age of Plenty* (New Haven, CT: Yale University Press, 2000) http://www.davidmyers.org/paradox/chapter1.html (12 June 2004).

10. Robert Bernstein, "Poverty, Income See Slight Changes; Child Poverty Rate Unchanged, Census Bureau Reports," US Census Bureau, 26 September 2003.

CHAPTER 2

1. Juliet Schor, *The Overworked American: The Unexpected Decline of Leisure* (New York: Basic Books, 1992), p. 114.

2. Ibid., p. 9.

3. Worldwatch Institute, "State of the World 2004: Consumption By the Numbers," http://www.worldwatch.org/press/news/2004/01/07/ (1 April 2004).

4. "Qualities That Drive Young to Succeed Also Lead to High Blood Pressure: Impatience, Hostility Make Unhealthy Mix," *USA Today*, 22 October 2003 http://www.psycport.com/stories/usatoday_2003_10_22_eng-usatoday_life_ eng-usatoday_life_051626_28751997152756737s11.xml.html (1 March 2004).

5. Schor, p. 11.

6. The cycle of work-and-spend, as Schor describes it: "Employers ask for long hours. The pay creates a high level of consumption. People buy houses and go into debt; luxuries become necessities; Smiths keep up with the Joneses. Each year, 'progress,' in the form of annual productivity increases, is doled out by employers as extra income rather than as time off." Schor, pp. 9–10.

7. Jessica Williams, *50 Facts That Should Change the World* (Cambridge: Icon Books, 2004), p. 133.

8. Ibid., p. 131.

9. Worldwatch Institute, "State of the World 2004: Consumption by the Numbers."

10. McCann-Erickson U.S. Advertising Volume Reports and Bob Coen's Insider's Report for December 2001, ww.mccann.com/insight/bobcoen.html (5 August 2002) and US Census Reports, all cited by the Center for a New American Dream, "Just the Facts about Advertising and Marketing to Children," http://www.newdream.org/campaign/kids/facts.html (15 May 2004).

11. Affluenza: PBS Program on the Epidemic of Overconsumption, "What Is It?" Diagnosis, http://www.pbs.org/kcts/affluenza/diag/what.html (2 April 2004).

12. Will Ferguson, *Happiness*™ (Toronto: Penguin Canada, 2002), p. 193.

13. David G. Myers, *The Pursuit of Happiness* (New York: Avon Books, 1993), p. 54.

14. David G. Myers, "Happiness," excerpted from *Psychology*, 7th Edition (New York: Worth Publishers, 2004), http://www.davidmyers.org/happiness/Excerpt.html (12 June 2004).

15. John de Graff et al., *Affluenza: The All-Consuming Epidemic* (San Francisco: Berrett-Koehler Publishers Inc., 2002), p. 13.

16. Ibid.

17. David Suzuki, *The Sacred Balance* (Toronto: Douglas & McIntyre, 2002), p. 23.

18. De Graff et al., p. 13.

19. David Gibson (RNS), "Is the New Christianity No Longer about 'We' and All about 'Me'?" *Salt Lake Tribune*, 15 January 2000.

20. De Graff et al., p. 13.

21. Eric Wieffering, "10 Years Later, the Mall of America Still Stands Alone," *Star Tribune*, http://www.startribune.com/viewers/story.php?template=print_a&'story=3133253 (1 April 2004).

22. Ibid.

23. Mall of America, "Media: History of MOA," http://www.mallofamerica.com/about_the_mall/moa_history.aspx (2 April 2004).

24. Jean Chatzky, *You Don't Have to be Rich: Comfort, Happiness and Financial Security on Your Own Terms* (New York: Portfolio/Penguin Books, 2003), p. 18.

25. Ibid. "People who earn around $50,000 a year are just as happy with their friendships, standard of living, marriage, children, and appearance as those who earn more than $100,000 a year."

26. Ibid., p. 36.

27. Worldwatch Institute, "State of the World 2004: Consumption by the Numbers."

28. Jonathan Power, "Nigeria: Happiest Nation on Earth?" *The Toronto Star*, 29 December 2003.

29. Affluenza: PBS Program on the Epidemic of Overconsumption, "What Is It?" Diagnosis.

30. Alfie Kohn, "In the Pursuit of Affluence, at a High Price," *The New York Times*, 2 February 1999.

CHAPTER 3

1. "Better Together," The Saguaro Seminar on Civic Engagement in America, December 2000, p. 76. The Saguaro Seminar on Civic Engagement in America is an ongoing initiative of Professor Robert D. Putnam at the John F. Kennedy School of Government at Harvard University.

2. Ibid., p. 5.

3. Robert Putnam, *Bowling Alone: The Collapse and Revival of American Community* (New York: Simon & Schuster, 2000), p. 204.

4. "Better Together," p. 3.

5. Putnam, p. 211.

6. George Ritzer elaborates this phenomenon in his seminal work, *The McDonalization of Society*. In relation to Max Weber's classic sociological

concept of "the irrationality of rationality," he explains that, "Contrary to McDonald's propaganda and the widespread belief in it, fast-food restaurants and their rational clones are not reasonable, or even truly rational systems. They spawn problems for the health of their customers and the well-being of the environment; they are dehumanizing and, therefore, unreasonable; and they often lead to the opposite of what they are supposed to create, for example, inefficiency rather than increased efficiency. None of this denies the advantages of McDonalization, but these examples clearly indicate the counterbalancing and perhaps even overwhelming problems associated with this process." George Ritzer, *The McDonalization of Society* (Thousand Oaks, CA: Pine Forge Press, 1996), p. 142.

7. Presbyterian Church USA, "The Ubiquity of Modern TV and Other Facts to Ponder in a Mediated World," The Great Electronic Awakening, 2003 http://www.pcusa.org/ega/more/stats.htm (31 March 2004).

8. Affluenza: PBS Program on the Epidemic of Overconsumption, "What Is It?" Diagnosis, http://www.pbs.org/kcts/affluenza/diag/what.html (2 April 2004).

9. Jessica Williams, *50 Facts That Should Change the World* (Cambridge: Icon Books, 2004), p. 214.

10. Statistics Canada, "Canadian Community Health Survey: Mental Health and Well-Being," 2002, http://stcwww.statcan.ca/english/sdds/3226.htm (1 March 2004).

11. Charles Derber, interview by the authors, 15 May 2003.

12. Dr. Jonathan White, *Hungry to Be Heard: Voices of Malnourished America*. Forthcoming, Oxford University Press.

13. Douglas Porpora, *How Holocausts Happen* (Philadelphia, PA: Temple University Press, 1990), pp. 24–25.

14. Andrew Palamarchuk, "TTC Driver Recovering After Attack: None of the More Than 20 Passengers on Bus Helped as Driver Was Beaten," *The Toronto Star*, 17 March 2004.

15. John Darley and Bibb Latané, "Bystander Intervention in Emergencies: Diffusion of Responsibility," *Journal of Personality and Social Psychology* 10 (1968): 202–214.

16. J.M. Darley and C.D. Batson, "From Jerusalem to Jericho": A Study of Situational and Dispositional Variables in Helping Behavior," *Journal of Personality and Social Psychology* 27 (1973): 100–108.

CHAPTER 4

1. Rev. Scott W. Alexander, "The Pursuit of Happiness," Sermon 57, 6 February 2000, http://www.rruc.org/sermon57.htm (12 June 2004).

CHAPTER 5

1. "... the people brought to Jesus all the sick and demon-possessed ... Jesus healed many who had various diseases. He also drove out many demons ..." Mark 1:32–34.

2. Matthew 4:23–25; Matthew 8:1–17.

3. Matthew 8:18.

4. Mishna Avot 1:14.

5. Mishna Torah 10:7–14.

6. "Invite (all) to the Way of thy Lord with wisdom and beautiful preaching; and argue with them in ways that are best and most gracious." *Qur'an,* Surah 16. The Bee (Al Nahl), Verse 125.

7. Al Ma'oon 107:1–7.

8. All quotes reflecting the Ethic of Reciprocity were cited from Golden Rule Poster by Paul McKenna, Scarboro Missions, 2000.

9. The Dalai Lama, *The Path to Tranquility: Daily Meditations,* ed. Renuka Singh (New York: Penguin, 2002), p. 10.

10. Plato suggested that the best possible political communities were those in which people were willing and able to be open to possibilities presented by others, and be willing to learn from others–because it is only in these communities that the possibility for the "best life" (and so the greatest happiness) for individuals exists.

11. Among the earliest philosophies to emphasize the balance between caring for the self and others are those of the 6th century B.C. philosophers Confucius and Lao Tzu, reputed author of the Tao Te Ching (The Way and Its Power). The Tao teaches that we should be humble and peaceful in our dealings with others: we learn best and help others learn when we listen to and respect the wisdom of others, and we contribute to our own peacefulness and the peacefulness of our community when we avoid contention and strive to resolve issues through peaceful means. Confucianism reflects much of the spirit of the Tao, but is much more explicitly concerned with the social, with one's conduct in the world. According to Confucius, friendship is central to one's development as a human being; good friendships result in the betterment of both friends. One cannot, therefore, strictly distinguish between what is good for oneself and what is good for one's community–these "goods" are one and the same.

12. Al-Farabi states that the best citizens will actively seek to develop the best virtues of others, and in so doing will become more virtuous themselves. In other words, in helping others, they become the best that they can be, and one becomes even better oneself. And, of course, the community as a whole becomes better. Everyone benefits.

13. Smith argues that the pursuit of individual self-interest under competitive conditions can foster a happy social order in which economic benefits are ("invisibly," through the workings of the market) widely distributed throughout that society.

14. Smith was concerned with the social, political, and moral consequences of economic activities in commercial societies. As David Korten argued in his book *When Corporations Rule the World,* "Smith believed the efficient market is composed of small, owner-managed enterprises located in the communities where the owners reside. Such owners normally share in the community's values and have a personal stake in the future of both the community and the enterprise." David C. Korten, "The Betrayal of Adam Smith," excerpt from *When Corporations Rule the World* (West Hartford, Conn: Kumarian Press, 2001) http://www.pcdf.org/corprule/betrayal.htm (12 June 2004).

15. Quoted in Tom Butler-Bowdon, *50 Self-Help Classics* (London: Nicholas Brealey Publishing, 2003), p. 145.

16. Ibid., p. 273.

17. Ibid.

18. Andrew Neher, "Maslow's Theory of Motivation: A Critique," *Journal of Humanistic Psychology* 31 (3) (1991): 89–112.

19. Members follow a 12-step program. Individuals must take the first few steps on their own, coming to the personal realization that they are powerless over alcohol and that its hold on life has become unmanageable. Although these first steps involve a personal discovery and commitment, members are not alone. AA recognizes a key facet of the healing process: that helping others is fundamental to an individual's own healing. A general principle is that conflict with or bad feeling toward others is an obstacle to recovery, something that disempowers us because it disconnects us from a key source of strength—others. Step eight in the program therefore asks that members make a list of all persons they had harmed, and become willing to make amends to all of them. Step nine requires them to make direct amends to such people whenever possible, except when to do so would injure them or others. And finally, in Step 12, having experienced a spiritual awakening as a result of the program, members begin to carry the healing message to other alcoholics in need of help.

CHAPTER 6

1. Jane Goodall, *In the Shadow of Man* (Boston: Houghton Mifflin Company, 1988), p. 248.

2. Modern sociology is largely built around the idea that the division of labor created by the industrial era—in which people split into increasingly segmented, specialized roles in society—explains the transition from "collective conscience" to a less socially cohesive functional interdependence. In short, the connection (or "solidarity") between members of society is no longer based on a sense of communal attachment, but on the increasingly self-interested premise that each person depends on another for a specific task. If the farmer no longer works the land, no one eats. If the carpenter no longer builds, no one has shelter. In his *The Division of Labour in Society* (1893), renowned sociologist Emile Durkheim outlined the transition from "mechanical solidarity" that connects a community through a *collective conscience* to "organic solidarity," connecting community through functional interdependence, brought on by the increasing division of labor in the industrial era. He also argued that the decline of the *collective conscience* led to the blurring of morality as individuals became less submerged in the community and more assigned to a specific role. "Even those systems with a highly developed organic solidarity still needed a common faith, a common *collective conscience,* if they were not to disintegrate into a heap of mutually antagonistic and self-seeking individuals." Lewis A. Coser, *Masters of Sociological Thought: Ideas in Historical and Social Context* (New York: Harcourt Brace Jovanovich College Publishers, 1977), pp. 129–132.

3. Durkheim coined the term "anomie" to define this phenomenon. Durkheim's *The Division of Labour in Society* (1893) and *Suicide* (1897) are considered seminal works in modern sociology. Some good secondary commentary is found in Murray State University's L. Joe Dunman, *Emile Durkheim Archive* (http://durkheim.itgo.com/main.html), and University of Illinois's Robert Alun Jones, *The Durkheim Pages* (http://www.relst.uiuc.edu/durkheim/).

4. But are we *really* predisposed to community and cooperation? Sigmund Freud's famous response to Albert Einstein's question, "Is there any way to deliver mankind from the menace of war," was that competition, and logically war, are instinctive to human nature, and that only by appealing to the individual's rational self-interest (that competition and war are counterproductive) can cooperation and peace be sustainably achieved. [Sigmund Freud, "Why War?" in *The Collected Papers*, ed. James Strachey (Basic Books, 1959)]. Margaret Mead's comment was that *War Is Only an Invention—Not a Biological Necessity.* [Margaret Mead, *Warfare Is Only an Invention—Not a Biological Necessity* (Asia: XL, 1940), pp. 402–405.] There have been hundreds

of studies—perhaps best encapsulated by Alfie Kohn in his *No Contest: The Case against Competition*—that demonstrate the existence of human tendencies toward cooperation and altruism that call into question the inherent nature of human selfishness. Kohn even capably debunks the myth that competition is superior to cooperation in terms of fostering higher productivity and progressive creativity through a survey of hundreds of studies showing the opposite. (Alfie Kohn, *No Contest: The Case against Competition* (Boston: Houghton Mifflin Company, 1986).

5. Quoted in William A. Galston, "Does the Internet Strengthen Community?" In *Democracy.com? Governance in a Networked World,* ed. Elaine Ciulla Kamarck and Joseph S. Nye, Jr. (Hollis, NH: Hollis 1999), http://www.puaf.umd.edu/IPPP/fall1999/internet_community.htm (15 May 2004).

6. M. Scott Peck, *The Different Drum* (New York: Simon & Schuster, 1987), quoted in Paul Rogat Loeb, *Soul of a Citizen* (New York: St. Martin's Press, 1999), p. 215.

7. John Kretzmann and John McKnight, *Building Communities from the Inside Out: A Path Toward Finding and Mobilizing a Community's Assets* (Chicago: ACTA Publication, 1998), quoted in Frank Riessman, "Ten Self-Help Principles," *Perspectives* 3 (2) http://mentalhelp.net/poc/view_doc.php?type=doc&id=358 (24 June 2004).

8. Community is not just about potlucks and get-togethers. It's about participation in the shaping of community. Robert D. Bellah argues that "Community is not about silent consensus; it is a form of intelligent, reflective life, in which there is indeed consensus, but where the consensus can be challenged and changed—often gradually, sometimes radically—over time." (Robert D. Bellah, "Community Properly Understood: A Defense of 'Democratic Communitarianism,'" *The Responsive Community* 6 (1) (Winter 1995/96) http://www.gwu.edu/~icps/bellah.html (15 May 2004). "[Democratic communitarianism] affirms the central value of solidarity, [which] points to the fact that we become who we are through our relationships; that reciprocity, loyalty, and shared commitment to the good are defining features of a fully human life." Participation in a democratic community is "both a right and a duty." Ibid.

CHAPTER 7

1. Viktor E. Frankl, *Man's Search for Meaning* (New York: Simon & Schuster, 1963), p. 104.

2. Ibid., p. 122.

3. Ibid., p. 58.

4. David G. Myers, "Happiness," excerpted from *Psychology*, 7th Edition (New York: Worth Publishers, 2004) http://www.davidmyers.org/happiness/Excerpt.html (9 June 2004).

5. The Famous Five included Emily Murphy, Henrietta Muir Edwards, Louise McKinney, Irene Parlby, and Nellie McClung. Between 1927–1929, they successfully fought for the right of women in Canada to be recognized as "persons" and thus able to serve in the Canadian Senate.

CHAPTER 8

1. The Dalai Lama and Howard C. Cutler, *The Art of Happiness: A Handbook for Living* (New York: Riverhead Books, 1998), p. 153.

CHAPTER 9

1. Phyllis Moen in a speech delivered at Cornell University, April 30, 1998. Quoted in Susan Lang, "Study: Volunteering Has Its Benefits For Those in Later Midlife. Professor Phyllis Moen speaks at the 'National Forum on Life Cycles and Volunteering' in Statler Auditorium April 30," *Cornell Chronicle*, 7 May 1998, www.news.cornell.edu/Chronicle/98/5.7.98/volunteering.html (2 December 2003). Professor Moen holds the McKnight Presidential Chair in Sociology at the University of Minnesota. Her research focuses on life-course transitions related to work, family, health, age, and gender stratification, and social policy.

2. We have collaborated a great deal with the YPO, an international network of presidents of corporations who are all under the age of 50. It includes some of the largest companies around the world.

3. The Body Shop, "Anita Roddick, OBE," n.d., http://www.thebodyshop.com/web/tbsgl/about_people_who_anita.jsp (29 March 2004).

4. David Macfarlane, "Corporate Social Responsibility," *Report on Business* 20 (9) March 2004, Cover.

5. GlobeScan is "a public opinion and stakeholder research firm that specializes in corporate issues." Statistics from its annual Corporate Social Responsibility Monitor are cited in Macfarlane, "Corporate," p. 46.

6. Mary Lynn Hemphill, "Volunteer For Your Health," *Peer Counseling Perspectives: Survival News*, April 2003, http://www.mindspring.com/~asp?SurvivalNews/April2003/peerscounsvol foryourhealth.htm (7 November 2003).

7. Health Canada, "Volunteering as a Vehicle for Social Support and Life Satisfaction," n.d., www.hc-sc.gc.ca/hppb/voluntarysector/benefits/benefits1a.html (7 November 2003).

8. Ibid. These claims are confirmed in a review of scientific studies published in the respected journal *Science* on 29 July 1988, suggesting that a "lack of social relationships constitutes a major risk factor for health that rivals in importance the effects of such well-established health factors as cigarette smoking, blood pressure, blood lipids, exercise, and obesity." In the words of Allan Luks and Peggy Payne, *The Healing Power of Doing Good: The Health and Spiritual Benefits of Helping Others* (New York: Fawcett Columbine, 1992), p. 3, describing the article by James House et al., "Social Relationships and Health," *Science*, 29 July 1988, p. 541.

9. L. Graff, *Volunteer for the Health of It* (Etobicoke, ON: Volunteer Ontario, 1991) http://www.hc-sc.gc.ca/hppb/voluntarysector/benefits/benefits2d.html (7 November 2003).

10. Allan Luks and Peggy Payne, *The Healing Power of Doing Good: The Health and Spiritual Benefits of Helping Others* (New York: Fawcett Columbine, 1992), p. 31.

11. Meredith Minkler, "People Need People: Social Support and Health," in *The Healing Brain: A Scientific Reader*, ed. Robert Ornstein and Charles Swencionis (New York: The Guilford Press, 1990), pp. 88–97.

12. Ibid., based on a 1979 Berkeley study.

13. Luks and Payne, *The Healing Power*, p. 7.

14. Ibid., p. 10.

15. Physiologically, it reduces stress and tension and breaks the cycle of negative effects caused by emotional stressors on physical well-being, such as high blood pressure and muscle tension. Moreover, the endorphins are natural opiates that relieve pain by interfering with the release of "Substance P," the body's chemical transmitter of pain messages to the brain.

16. In surveys, respondents told Luks that during this time, they had feelings of increased self-worth, greater happiness and optimism, and a decrease in helplessness and depression. And these effects are experienced each time the act of helping was remembered by the volunteer. It is thus the absence of bad feelings, combined with the presence of good feelings, that helping provides.

17. Luks and Payne, p. 16.

18. Ibid., 38.

19. Ibid., 68.

20. Quoted in Luks and Payne, 68.

21. Mark Bricklin et al., *Positive Living and Health: The Complete Guide to Brain/Body Healing and Mental Empowerment* (Emmaus, PA: Rodale Press, 1989) p. 115.

22. S.L. Bruhn and S. Wolf, "Update on Roseto, Pennsylvania: Testing a Prediction," *Psychosomatic Medicine* 40 (1978): 86.

23. American Heart Association, "Heart Facts 2003: All Americans," n.d., http://www.americanheart.org/downloadable/ heart/1046365800849HFAAFS.pdf (16 May 2004).

24. M.A. Musick and J. Wilson, "Volunteering and Depression: The Role of Psychological and Social Resources in Different Age Groups," *Social Science and Medicine* 56 (2003): 259–269.

    N. Morrow-Howell et al., "Effects of Volunteering on the Well-Being of Older Adults," *Journals of Gerontology: Series B: Psychological Sciences & Social Sciences* 58B (3) (2003): S137–S145.

    M.A. Musick, R. Herzog, and J.S. House, "Volunteering and Mortality among Older Adults: Findings from a National Sample," *The Journals of Gerontology* 54B (3) (1999): S173–S180.

    C. Davis et al., "Benefits to Volunteers in a Community-Based Health Promotion and Chronic Illness Self-Management Program for the Elderly," *Journal of Gerontological Nursing* 24 (10) (1998): 16–23.

25. Lang, "Study: Volunteering Has Its Benefits For Those in Later Midlife," *Cornell Chronicle.*

26. S.L. Brown et al., "Providing Social Support May Be More Beneficial Than Receiving It: Results from a Prospective Study of Mortality," *Psychological Science* 14 (4) (2003): 320–327.

27. The Take Action series currently includes: (1) *Take Action! A Guide to Active Citizenship,* Toronto: Gage, 2002 (early high school) (2) *Take More Action,* Toronto: Nelson, 2004 (late high school / early college). Note: *Take Action Adventures* (forthcoming).

28. Bricklin et al., p. 114.

29. James Youniss et al., "The Role of Community Service in Identity Development: Normative, Unconventional, and Deviant Orientations," *Journal of Adolescent Research* 14 (2) (1999): 248–261.

30. Cynthia W. Moore and Joseph P. Allen, "The Effects of Volunteering on the Young Volunteer," *The Journal of Primary Prevention* 17 (2) (1996): 231.

31. Joseph Allen et al., "Preventing Teen Pregnancy and Academic Failure: Experimental Evaluation of a Developmentally Based Approach," *Child Development* 64 (4) (1997): 729–742, as cited in Jessica Portner, "Volunteerism Reduces Teen Pregnancy, Study Finds," *Education Week on the Web,* 10 September 1997, <http://www.edweek.org/ew/vol-17/02teen.h17> (29 March 2004).

CHAPTER 10

1. Brian Murphy, *Transforming Ourselves, Transforming the World* (New York: Zed Books, 1999), p. 20.

2. Bill Moyer et al., *Doing Democracy: The Map Model for Organizing Social Movements* (Gabriola Island, BC: New Society Publishers, 2001), p. 2.

3. Howard Zinn, *You Can't Be Neutral on a Moving Train* (Boston: Beacon Press, 1994), pp. 83–84.

4. Harriet Taylor is generally credited with co-authoring several of her husband John Stuart Mill's essays on the right of women to political participation in the late 1840s and early 1850s, including *The Enfranchisement of Women*.

5. Frederick Douglass was a key figure in the American abolitionist movement over the two decades leading to the Civil War. He escaped from slavery, joined the Massachusetts Anti-Slavery Society, and fled to England before returning to buy his freedom and lead the political charge for the Thirteenth Amendment.

6. Jody Williams shared the 1997 Nobel Peace Prize with the International Campaign to Ban Landmines, the organization she helped to found in 1991.

7. One of the greatest living human beings in the world. Seriously, if you don't know who Nelson Mandela is by now, please immediately put this book down and rush out to the library to read *A Long Walk to Freedom*.

8. The civil rights movement itself was grounded in centuries of turmoil and perseverance from the days of slavery to the pivotal *Brown v. Board of Education* case against school segregation in 1954, to all of the other battles, big and small, that have been waged for this cause over many years.

9. Bonnie Eisenberg and Mary Ruthsdofter, "Living the Legacy: The Women's Rights Movement, 1848–1988," The National Women's History Project, 1988, http://www.legacy98.org/move-hist.html (May 16, 2004).

10. This is a variation of the "Mutually Hurting Stalemate" conceived by William Zartman. He found that negotiations started when parties reached a point in the conflict when both sides were hurting and neither side could unilaterally change the status quo. William Zartman, "Ripeness: The Hurting Stalemate and Beyond," in *International Conflict Resolution after the Cold War*, Committee on International Conflict Resolution, ed. Paul C. Stern and Daniel Druckman (Washington, DC: National Research Council, 2000), p. 225.

CHAPTER 11

1. Katherine Macklem, "Top 100 Employers: The Best Employers Do More Than Issue Paycheques. They Improve Life in the Workplace and in the

Surrounding Community as Well," *Macleans,* 20 October 2003, http://www.macleans.ca/webspecials/article.jsp?content=20031020_67488_67488 (12 March 2004).

2. Job sharing occurs when the duties and responsibilities of a position are shared between two people.

3. Schor, *The Overworked American,* p. 163.

4. For information on the impact of this program, see http://www.aidmatrix.com/home.jsp.

5. Art DeFehr quoted by Madelaine Drohan, "The Faith That Dare Not Speak Its Name," *Report on Business* 20 (6), December 2003, p. 68.

6. Quoted in John F. Raynolds and Eleanor Raynolds, *Beyond Success: How Volunteer Service Can Help You Begin Making a Life Instead of Just a Living* (New York: MasterMedia Limited, 1988.), p. 22.

7. Jubilee 2000 is a remarkable campaign that unites various religious organizations and institutions around the world to help eliminate the debt of the world's poorest countries. More information is available at http://www.jubileeusa.org.

8. A remarkable campaign for young people (and youth of all ages) originally developed by Sports for Hunger.

9. Quoted from Simon Moll of The Otesha Project. For more information about the organization, see http://www.otesha.ca.

10. Marian Wright Edelman (b. 1943) is a prolific author, lecturer, and social activist for disadvantaged Americans. In 1973, she established the Children's Defense Fund, a powerful voice for children and families in the United States, with a mission to "Leave no child behind."

CHAPTER 12

1. UNESCO Institute for Statistics, "Regional Adult Illiteracy Rate and Population by Gender: July Year 2002 Assessment," Literacy and Non-Formal Education Sector, 2002, www.uis.unesco.org/en/stats/statistics/UIS_Literacy_Regional2002.xls (16 May 2004).

2. This theory is not based on the fact that we all have an abundance of natural resources awaiting our consumption (and the further destruction of our environment), but rather that we have an abundance of gifts, talents, energy, and passion to share with the world.

Index

A

advertising, 19

"Advice," as best-seller category, 6

Affluenza: The All-Consuming Epidemic, 20

Aga Khan, 179

Agnes, 1–2

Aidmatrix, 173

Alcoholics Anonymous, 75

Alexander, Scott W., 57

Al-Farabi, 72

Allen, Joseph P., 145

altruism, 97

An Inquiry into the Nature and Causes of the Wealth of Nations, 72

Andes Mountains, 82

Andrew, 49, 50

Angel Network, 22–23

"asset-based development," 122

Avner, Lindsay, 165–168, 192

B

balancing self and other, 123–125, 183

Bedouins, 70–71

Ben and Jerry's, 138

Bender, Thomas, 92

Bill, 31–33

Black and Decker, 172

bodhicitta (compassion), 78

Body Shop, 22, 138, 172

Bono, 22

Bowling Alone, 33–34

branding, 19

Buckley, Kathy, 127–131

Building Communities from the Inside Out, 93

business success, 138–139

"bystander effect," 40–41

C

Callwood, June, 175–176

Carlos, Pedro, 66, 67

Carter, Jimmy, 179

Chatzky, Jean, 21

child labor, 50–55

chimpanzees, 97

Christine, 118–119

Christmas Kindness South Africa
2002, 114–115

civil rights movement, 158–159

"collective conscience," 88, 89

community service, 137, 139

community
 and balance, 123
 and competition, 56
 and connectedness, 36–37
 and happiness, 57–59
 and social change, 174–178
 and suffering, 120
 creating, 81, 92
 evolution of, 87–88
 rebuilding, 81

compassion, 118–119

competition, 37

Confucius, 72

Craig, 50–53

cross, as symbol, 19

D

Dalai Lama, 70, 77–78, 195

Davos, Switzerland, 15, 16

de Tocqueville, Alexis, 174

DeFehr, Art, 173

Delaney, Chris, 104–105

Democracy in America, 174

Democratic Communitarianism, 94

Derber, Charles, 37

Direct Energy, 172

Douglass, Frederick, 74, 158

Durkheim, Emile, 88, 89

E

Ecuador, 82, 121

Edelman, Marian Wright, 184

Einstein, Albert, 73

Eismann, Edward, 145

Emerson, Ralph Waldo, 111

Ethic of Reciprocity, 68–69

F

faith group and social change,
 178–180

family and social change, 170–172

Famous Five, 110

Ferguson, Will, 19

forgiveness, 118–120

Fox, Terry, 196, 109

Frankl, Victor, 102–103

Franklin, Benjamin, 15, 72–73

Free the Children
 and balance, 124
 and economic forum, 15
 and social movements, 159–163
 and volunteers, 136
 and workers, 194
 in Afghanistan, 95
 in Brazil, 197
 in China, 125
 in Ecuador, 38

in North America, 135
in San Francisco, 182
in Sierra Leone, 74, 142
origin, 51, 53
Freetown, Sierra Leone, 118

G
Gabriel, Peter, 22
Gaither, Dorothea, 89, 119
Gaither, John, 147–149, 152, 192
Gandhi, Mahatma, 109, 196
Genovese, Catherine, 40
Gere, Richard, 77–80
"gifted" people, 193–195
gifts, sharing, 196–197
Girl in the Picture, 11, 14
Gladwell, Malcolm, 164
Goodall, Jane, 97–98, 192
goodwill, 58
gratitude journal, 106
Great Rift Valley, 84
Ground Zero, 94, 95
Guinea, 99

H
Halloween for Hunger, 182–183
Hansen, Rick, 196
happiness, defining, 4–5, 107
Harpo, Inc., 114
"Healthy Helping Phenomenon," 141
"Helper's High," 141
Hetrick, Sonya, 134
Hewlett-Packard, 172

hierarchy of needs, 74
Hillel, Rabbi, 161
Holocaust, 102
Homo habilis, 84
"hurting stalemate," 163–164
Huse, James, 140

I
inertia, 155–156, 161, 164
Inez, Kentucky, 95

J
Jewel, 22
Johnstone, Emma, 149–153
Johnstone, Gord, 151–152
Johnstone, Jan, 151–152
José, 198–199

K
Kennedy, Robert, 185
Kenya, 84
Kim Foundation, 14
King, Martin Luther
    and conscience, 176
    and faith, 162
    and inter-faith coalitions, 180
    and success, 109
    speech, 158
Klong Toey, Bangkok, 90–92, 107
Kretzmann, John, 93

L
Lao Tzu, 72, 157
Leakey, Louis, 84, 97

Leakey, Mary, 84

Lefens, Tim, 43–46

Lemay, Oliver, 134

Levi-Strauss, 172

Lewin, Lowell, 141

Lincoln, Abraham, 73

Llilla, Ecuador, 152

Luks, Allan, 140–141

Lusseyran, Jacques, 119

M

Macdonald's, 19

Mafinder family, 99–102

Mall of America, 20–21

Man's Search for Meaning, 102

Mandela, Nelson
  and faith, 162
  and Oprah Winfrey, 114
  and Rivonia Trial, 158
  and success, 109, 110
  contributions, 196

Marc, 48–50

March on Washington, 158

Maria, 49, 50

Masai Mara, 84–85

Masai tribe, 84–86, 94

Maslow, Abraham, 73–74

material success, 17–18

McClelland, David, 141

McKnight, John, 93

"Me Generation," 8, 47

Me to We Club, 176–177

Mel, 97

minga, 82–83

Mishna, 67–68

Missionaries of Charity, 2

Modest Needs, 26–28

Moen, Phyllis, 135. 143, 177

money, and happiness, 21–22

Moore, Cynthia W., 145

Mother Teresa
  and faith, 178
  and prayer, 123–124
  and success, 110
  contributions, 196
  in Calcutta, 3–5, 10

"Mother Teresa syndrome," 4

Movement Action Plan, 157

Moyer, Bill, 157

Muniannal, 52

Myers, David, 105–106

N

Nagashir, 53–55, 59

"need-based development," 122

Negev Desert, 71

Newman, Paul, 22

Newton, Isaac, 73

Niemöller, Martin, 42

9/11, 94, 95

Nobel, Alfred, 110–111

Nobel Prize, 110–111

O

Opatowski, Joe, 187–190

P

Parks, Rosa, 109, 110, 158–159, 162

partnership vs charity, 121, 122

Paul, Alice, 159

Paul Newman salad dressings, 138

Peck, M. Scott, 93

Perl, Fritz, 8

personal identity, 88

Phuc, Kim, 11–14

Pi-Jai, 91

Plato, 71

poverty, 56

prayer, 78–79

Puruhae, 94, 82–83, 84, 121–122

Putnam, Robert, 33–34

Q

Qur'an, 68

R

Race for the Cure–High School Challenge, 168

Ramirez, 49, 50

Rato Monastery, 78

reality television, 38

reconciliation, 118–119

Riverton, Jamaica, 188–190

Rivonia Trial, 158

Roddick, Anita, 22, 138

Roosevelt, Eleanor, 73–74

Roots and Shoots, 98

Roseto, Pennsylvania, 141–142

Rotary Clubs, 137–138

Run for the Cure, 167

Ryan, Richard, 20

S

Salvador, Brazil, 197

Sander, Allison, 134–135

Schor, Juliet, 18

Schweitzer, Albert, 74, 105

Scott, 49, 50

self-help, roots of, 59, 65

self-help books, 7, 8

self-help culture

and consumerism, 23

and detachment, 40

and happiness, 31, 33

and materialism, 9, 10

and social fabric, 37

and societal shift, 58

and success, 17

charting new path in, 47–48

escaping, 84, 85

self-help industry, 6–7, 8

Self-Help, 73

Shell, 19

Sierra Leone, West Africa, 74–75, 99, 142–143

Singh, Lekha, 173

Sisters, the, 142–143

"Slaughter House" district, Klong Toey, 91

Smiles, Samuel, 73

Smith, Adam, 72

social decline, 34, 35–36

social identity, 88–89

social inertia, 155

social isolation, 140

social movements, 157, 160–161, 182

social support, 142

Spindle, 97

Stanton, Elizabeth Cady, 159

Storming of the Bastille, 158

street children, 197–199

success, defining, 4–5, 109

Suicide, 89

Survivor, 38–39, 47

T

Take Action!, 144

Taylor, Harriet, 158

Taylor, Keith, 25–29

Teen Outreach, 145

television, 35–36

The Art of Virtue, 73

Theory of Moral Sentiments, 72

Tipping Point, 164

Torah, 68

TRW Vidar, 172

Tutu, Desmond, 61–62

tzedakah (righteous deeds), 68

U

Union Fire Company, 73

UNITAS, 145

"unity, fellowship and service," 75–76

Ut, Nick, 12

V

voice, 183–184

Volunteer Now, 144, 145

volunteering

    and health, 143–144

    and relationships, 136

    and students, 144–146

vote, 183–184

Vreeland, Nicky, 78

W

Waslala, Nicaragua, 66

"We Generation," 47

Weiss, Jordan, 149–153

Wells Fargo, 172

White, Jonathan, 62–63

Wieffering, Eric, 20

Williams, Jessica, 19

Williams, Jody, 158

Winfrey, Oprah, 22–23, 113–115

women's rights movement, 159

workplace and social change, 172–174

World Economic Forum, 15, 16

World Values Survey, 22

X

Xerox, 172

Xiuyan county, China, 125

Y

York, Peter, 7

Young Presidents' Organization, 138

youth and social change, 180–182

Z

zakat (charity), 68

zebras, 86–87

Zinn, Howard, 158

LIBRARY
NSCC, WATERFRONT CAMPUS
80 MAWIO'MI PLACE
DARTMOUTH, NS B2Y 0A5 CANADA

DISCARDED

Still Want to Learn

JUL 2 7 2014

Date Due

BRODART, CO.   Cat. No. 23-233   Printed in U.S.A.

www.m_____ _____ _____s invaluable in_____ for people who wish to find the _____le to We philoso___ _____.

The site_____

- Insp_____ _____ and _____ _____ live the Me _____
- Spec_____ths, and senio__ on how to _____
- Tips _____ and _____
- Stati_____ed your help
- Link _____ es on a local, national, and international level.
- Discussion boards and chat rooms.
- Much, much more!

Log on today and take the next step to transform your own life through helping others.